I only eat BERTONI

Homemade Italian Food

By Albert and Anthony

NEW
HOLLAND

First published in 2010 by New Holland Publishers (Australia) Pty Ltd
Sydney • Auckland • London • Cape Town

www.newholland.com.au

1/66 Gibbes Street Chatswood NSW 2067 Australia
218 Lake Road Northcote Auckland New Zealand
86 Edgware Road London W2 2EA United Kingdom
80 McKenzie Street Cape Town 8001 South Africa

A record of this is available at the National Library of Australia.

ISBN: 9781741109689.

Publisher: Fiona Schultz
Publishing manager: Lliane Clarke
Photography: Karen Watson (recipes) and Emma Gough (incidentals)
Cover photograph: Emma Gough
Stylist: Georgie Dolling
Project editor: Talina McKenzie
Editor: Meryl Potter
Proofreader: Victoria Fisher
Designer: Emma Gough
Cover design: Emma Gough
Production manager: Olga Dementiev
Printer: Toppan Leefung Printing Limited (China)

I only eat BERTONI

Homemade Italian Food

This book is dedicated to our late brother Angelo,
who left this world way before his time.
We miss you every day.

toasted or fresh

olone. tomato
ovolone. tomato
. provolone. tomato
. provolone, eggplant
. tomato. pesto

Sml $6   Med $8   Lg $12

$8

Bertoni Pasta
Homemade Gnocchi
Ravioli + Tortellini
Lasagna $10

Meat dishes

o Slow baked stews
o Osso bucca
o Involtini
o Ripieni

(Seasonal)

	Med	Lge
	$10	$15
	$10	$15
	$10	$15
		15

...lloni $10

w/ side
...tballs
...les
...nitzel
...sts

Dolci

- Canoli $3
- Ciambella $4.50
- Sfogliatella $5.50
- Zuccherati $4.50
- Jam doughnut $4.50
- Biscotti
- Amaretti home made $3.00
- Jam hearts ....
- Cannella $4.00
- Romani $4.00
- Almond croissant $4.50
- Portuguese tart $3
- Smiley face $2.50

Caffe

- Caffe Reg $3.3
- Caffe Lg $4.0
- Hot choc Reg $3.3
           Lg $4.0
- Mocha Reg $4.0
          Lg $4.5
- Bertoni cold $3.
      caffe
- Bertoni latte $3.
  (doppio ristretto)

"Having Alberto and Antonio's family casalinga a healthy walking distance away from home in the heart of town means that we can pretend we are back in Bella Italia—at least for half an hour a day!

Whether it's their caffé or their cibo … it's just like the food and coffee-obsessed country and culture that have become our family's seconda paese. All that's missing is the cheap but drinkable half-litre of red, but most of us are tottering on our legendary Bertoni milk crates far too early for a vino rosso locale! Meanwhile, Mamma's recipes, affectionately and freshly replicated out the back, are the real thing. Come on. Be honest! How many of us have appeared to be merely eyeing off the piled-high daily platters of chunky panini, evil dolci, colourful insalati, authentic pasta sauces, clever wraps and those complementary meats, poultry etc., when the reality is we are actually trying to take a mental picture of each one so we can try and recreate them at home?"

George Negus

CONTENTS
Contenuto

Albert, Mamma and Anthony

INTRODUCTION
Proemio

Our café…

Since Albert and I were teenagers, we always talked about opening our own café or restaurant one day. We were always passionate about food and coffee, and would travel almost anywhere to find a good coffee, a traditional panino or a cannoli like the ones we'd had at our cousin's pasticceria in Sicily. Whenever we visited other cafés and restaurants Albert would be in my ear, 'Mate, if we owned this place can you imagine what we could do with it?'

When we started discussing the concept, Albert made it pretty clear that he didn't want to work nights as he was starting a family, so we brainstormed ideas for a daytime café and deli. After many discussions over many meals, espressos and even a grappa or two, we came up with the concept of what we wanted our place to be:

'A place where people would come and have a complete Italian experience, as they would if they were in Italy. Where everything was simple, the range was limited but the quality was exceptional. Where you could have a fresh panino and great coffee for not a lot of money. And when you walked in you would be greeted as if you were visiting an old family friend. Staff would know your name, smile and know what your regular order was.'

The Bertoni name came about over a coffee with a very good friend and former business associate, Gary Berger. We were discussing the new venture and brainstorming names (one of which was Salami Bros). He said 'Bert and Tony, there it is—Bertoni.' It was an instant hit and we all agreed it was a great name. Gary has often mentioned he should receive a royalty for the name, but instead we have agreed that he can drink as much coffee as he likes and eat as much lasagna as he can fit in. He seems to be OK with this arrangement.

And so it went. We had our concept and our name. We found a location, ran some projections and then signed our first lease in Balmain in Sydney's inner west. That was the start of Bertoni.

"Earliest childhood smells would be garlic frying in olive oil before the freshly diced garden tomatoes were added."

OUR FAMILY
La nostra famiglia

Our Dad arrived in Australia in 1951 by boat from Raffadali, in Sicily. He was working on the land in Sicily and his brother (our uncle Zio Nino) was already here and told him there was plenty of work. Our mother came from Santa Maria in Naples in 1957. They were introduced and married later that year.

Dad worked five and a half days a week in a factory, but most of his spare time was devoted to his backyard garden, or the 'family farm' as we used to call it. When we were growing up, there was always an abundance of beautiful, fresh food, and our meals were mostly determined by what was currently growing in the garden. The array of vegetables seemed endless—tomatoes, beans, zucchini (courgettes), eggplant (aubergine), baby carrots, potatoes, onions, garlic, fresh herbs and chilli. Dad also dabbled in growing fruit, including strawberries, lemons, mandarins, oranges, mangoes, plums, apricots, peaches and the lushest prickly pear fruit. In early years, we even had chickens in our backyard to supply fresh eggs and chicken meals.

The family farm wasn't limited to our Dad's garden, as each of our five uncles living in Australia also had their own backyard plantations, and tomatoes were always the primary production. One month before the seeds were planted, our Dad would meet with his brothers to discuss the seeds they were going to use for the current season. Some would have dried out seeds from last year's crop, while others would have a stash from someone's neighbour, the man down the street, or a man from the glass factory where they worked. The seeds were distributed amongst the brothers so they could all share in the bounty. Planting the seeds, nurturing the pots, transferring to the soil, staking the trunks, picking old leaves, and watering each and every afternoon would be tough work, but when the first tomatoes appeared they would be enjoyed by the family in a tomato, onion and cucumber salad. Finally the fruits of our labour would be rewarded.

An excess of tomatoes meant pasta sauce was made fresh daily. Earliest childhood smells would be garlic frying in olive oil before the freshly diced garden tomatoes were added and stirred. 'Albert, girra u suco', our mother would say, which was an instruction for the tallest child to stir the sauce to avoid it sticking to the saucepan. Mum's red sauce was then not only added to pasta dishes, but was also used for all meat bases, stews, stuffed capsicums, vegetable soups and even our poached eggs … mmmhhh!

Mum was a traditional Italian housewife who devoted her life to looking after her four children and her husband. She cooked, cleaned, disciplined, dressed, groomed, fed us and passed onto us her passion for food. Mum has always looked her happiest at a table surrounded by her family enjoying her food. There's always an extra secret ingredient that she's added to her dishes, which we quiz her about until she can no longer keep it in and like a little girl finally whispers, 'fresh oregano' or 'pork fat'.

Mum insists that she didn't know how to cook when she married Dad. In her words she even 'burnt water'. Her father, our nonno Alberto, was a chef and we truly believe she inherited her father's creative cooking gene, because she developed into the most amazing cook. Mum's theory was and still is that you should try all foods that exist, otherwise you'll never know what you're missing out on. We've eaten soup made with chicken heads and chicken feet, smoked frog's legs, snails, livers, kidneys, hearts, tripe and brains, just to name a few.

We remember many times in the mid-1970s, sitting around the kitchen table, Mum trying to muster support for her suggestion of opening an Italian restaurant and calling it Mamma Maria's. Dad would look at her in a way that only a 1950s husband could look at his wife, and destroy the only dream she ever had with that one look. All of us thought Mum was crazy—we could never open an Italian restaurant. 'She's losing it', we'd say. She said she would cook in the kitchen and us kids could take the orders from the customers. Mum was undaunted by the fact that her English was not great and her children were still young. She knew that her food was fresh, simple and homemade, and casalinga-style cooking was what people wanted. Thirty years later Bertoni opened. I guess Mum was just ahead of her time.

Bert...

Distinct smells emerged from the kitchen at different times of day when we were growing up.

First thing in the morning, it was an Italian espresso brewing before my father went to work.

7am: it's espresso and enough boiled eggs to feed four kids with toast, melted butter and mild coffee biscuits.

9am: the garlic is gently frying in the pot that will form the base of the sauce.

11am: the tomatoes have been cooking for more than two hours, and a sweet scent fills the house.

11.30am: fresh greens—radicchio, shallots, spinach and silverbeet—sautéed with garlic and onion, are slapped over day-old bread.

12noon: eggs are whisked and added to a gentle sauté of broad beans and baby onions, picked right at our doorstep.

3pm: eggs and sugar are poured into a bain-marie, and afternoon dessert is ready for the kids when they get home from school.

5pm: *Hogan's Heroes* starts, and the pasta is added to the pot. Dad will be home in fifteen minutes and we all need to be ready for the family dinner, which there is no excuse not to attend.

6pm: after two courses of pasta and meat, we are ready for a third course of fruit and nuts. All the nuts are still in their shell, so the family becomes proficient in the shelling and distribution process among a family of six. Even with nuts we were always taught fresh, unshelled is the best.

8pm: Mum serves up her sultana muffin cake, which is washed down with a cold caffè latte. This makes the house smell like a big sweet sultana muffin. If cake isn't your thing, another box, filled

*"This food ritual was repeated every day
… for more than twenty years."*

with Scotch Fingers, is offered with another caffè latte to go with your biscuits—why not?

This food ritual was repeated every day (with changes made to ensure variety) for more than twenty years.

Tony…

Looking back, growing up in an Italian family in the south-west of Sydney was good grounding for our future career. Everything we did involved coffee, food and family.

At school, Mum occasionally tried to help me integrate by making me vegemite or jam sandwiches (I was the youngest of four children so the others took a lot of the embarrassing hits before I was born). But although she limited the salami panini rolls filled with antipasto and parmesan cheese, she didn't stop coming to my school once a week and delivering my lunch. It wasn't so much the type of lunch she delivered— pizza, pasta or stuffed artichokes—it was the fact that she was waiting for me in the playground when I came out for lunch and she would set up a picnic and sit with me until I finished. Some of my friends would join me (she always made enough for ten people), but it didn't make it any less embarrassing. At that age, it just wasn't cool. I really hated these times, even though I really enjoyed the food.

When we were younger, our days at the beach were very similar. We would all get up early and pack the Esky full of water, beers, soft drinks and ice. Mum would be up at the same time and would prepare lunch: pizza, pasta, risotto, panini, dolci and fruit, to name just a few. At the beach we would meet at least three or four other families, usually my Dad's brothers and sisters with their kids, and we would occupy a large area on the sand either at Brighton or, on very special occasions, at Cronulla. We would swim until about 11am and then we would come out and get ready for lunch. By the time we put all the food out from all the families there was enough to feed a small army. We often got funny glaring looks from the other families at the beach, but at the time I wasn't sure what they were looking at. We would finish our feast off with some watermelon and homemade granita, and then pack up.

The worst part of the day was always after lunch, because our parents would make us wait for up to three hours before we were allowed to go swimming again. Apparently swimming on a full stomach caused stomach cramps. They always had the same story about the child who drowned because they went swimming too soon after eating lunch. We questioned this urban myth as our Australian friends would always swim right after food and nothing ever happened to them. But the argument would quickly come to a close with my Dad telling us to shut up and wait. And so we did.

The extended family...

Big celebrations were always shared with family, and everyone brought along their respective specialities.

Zio Giovanni would always prepare his fresh, spicy pork sausages. Zia Catarina's specialty was inbuliati—ten layers of dough layered with sausage or olives, drizzled with olive oil and fennel seeds. The adults would always comment on how good they tasted accompanied by a cold beer or red wine. Zia Emmanuella made her special macco—a broad bean soup made with garden-fresh beans. Zia Angela was the baker. She arrived in Australia when she was a baby and so she embraced the country's local desserts—sugared jam rolls, lamingtons, walnut cakes, fennel-seeded shortbread biscuits and cookies. As kids we would say, 'Where does she come from, and why doesn't Mum know how to bake cookies?' Zia Rosa's speciality was pizza, topped with garlic, olives, anchovies and fresh tomato. Mum would make salt-cured sardines. It took about four months to expel all the water, but this method created the sweetest-tasting sardines. We had a shared loaf of bread, which we would dip into a bowl of virgin olive oil, balsamic vinegar and oregano, and then top with the sardine. While Zia Maria did not have any speciality dishes as such, she always brought along an array of amazing fruit that was at least two to three times the size of conventional fruit. King Street, Newtown was the place to buy fruit in the early 1970s.

After the food, our parties usually involved moving the furniture back and dancing to the music of the era. It was not just a family celebration of whatever occasion it happened to be, it was a celebration of three brothers, three sisters, and their respective wives, husbands and families who immigrated to this country to find a better life. They were special times.

"Big celebrations were always shared with family, and everyone brought along their respective specialities."

"Our mother has always told us that the secret to great-tasting food was keeping it simple."

OUR FOOD
Il Nostro Cibo

Dad's been growing his own fruit and vegetables since he was a farmer back in Sicily, and when we were growing up, we always had a fresh selection of whatever was in season at the time. And still today, although he is in his early eighties, Dad spends most of his time in his backyard 'family farm'.

Mum has never used a store-bought pasta sauce—she has been making her own since before we were born. She learned how to make the sauce from her mother, who learned from her mother. It's one of those things that have been in the family forever.

Our mother has always told us that the secret to great-tasting food was keeping it simple and using the best and freshest ingredients. Mum and Dad's love and passion for fresh food were transferred to all of us as kids and they continue today. Our parents were the inspiration behind all the flavours of Bertoni.

When we started pulling together the recipes for this book, we ended up with a list too long to publish. So we've narrowed it down to a succinct selection of the classics, which includes the most popular dishes that we make fresh in our cafés every day and some of our own personal favourites from Mum's Sicilian–Neapolitan repertoire. We hope you'll enjoy making these dishes and eating them with your own families at home.

It was a real challenge getting Mum's recipes from her, as she's been cooking for more than fifty years and has never written a recipe down once. She has never measured ingredients, always adding on taste or feel, and rarely is a dish made exactly the same way twice. There's always a slight variation, but it always tastes great.

The ingredients throughout this book list some of Bertoni's pantry staples, such as our Sugo del Giardino (tomato sauce), Olio Verde (Sicilian green extra virgin olive oil) and Balsamic del Modena (vinegar). If you can't get these ingredients when making the dishes, you can replace with similar, high-quality products.

Buon appetito

PASTA, RISOTTO AND PIZZA

Pasta, risotti e pizza

*O*ur earliest memories of pasta would be playing in the shed and drawing on the side of stacked boxes filled with dried pasta that was bought on special from a local deli or supermarket. Feeding a large family on my father's factory wage was a challenge for my parents, so while pasta was in abundant supply, it was always economically purchased after reading an ad in the local Italian newspaper or getting a tip from an uncle on where to buy cheap bulk Italian supplies.

Like most Italian families, both here in Australia and in the motherland, we grew up with endless variations of pasta dishes. Our mother made all the classics and then mixed it up with new variations made of whatever came out of Dad's garden at the time.

We never had pasta as a meal on its own. It was always served as a first course lead in to the many courses that followed—and always served with freshly grated parmesan or pecorino cheese, and some crusty Italian bread bought from the deli early that day.

PASTA WITH BROCCOLINI

Orecchiette con broccolini

This dish has minimal ingredients and is so simple to make but the combination of the garlic, anchovies and chilli gives it real flavour. It is one of our Dad's favourite pasta dishes.

Preparation time 10 minutes
Cooking time 30 minutes
Serves 4

400g (13 oz) broccolini
500g (1 lb) dried orecchiette pasta*
125ml (½ cup, 4 fl oz) Olio Verde plus extra to drizzle**
4 cloves garlic, peeled and thinly sliced
8 marinated anchovies, drained and finely chopped
1 small red chilli, de-seeded and finely chopped

80g (7 tablespoons, 3 oz) grated parmesan cheese plus extra for serving
salt and pepper to taste plus a good pinch of salt for cooking the pasta

Cut the heads of the broccolini into small florets. Trim and thinly slice the stems. Bring a medium-sized pot of water to the boil over medium heat, add salt and blanch the broccolini for 3–4 minutes until soft. Drain well, reserving the cooking water.

Return the cooking water to the pot and bring it to the boil. Cook the pasta according to the packet instructions. Drain, retaining approximately 125ml (½ cup, 4 fl oz) of the water.

Heat the oil in a large frying pan over medium heat and add the garlic, anchovies and chilli, and cook, stirring, for 4 minutes or until the garlic is soft and the mixture is fragrant. Add the retained water and bring to the boil. Add the broccolini and pasta, and season to taste.

Remove from heat and stir in the parmesan.

Serve immediately with a drizzle of oil and the extra freshly grated parmesan cheese.

* Our recipe lists dried pasta as the ingredient but you can substitute homemade or store-bought fresh pasta available from gourmet food stores and selected grocers.
** See Basics.

MAMMA MARIA'S SPAGHETTI AND MEATBALLS
Pasta polpette alla Maria

We always wondered why our Mum's polpette were so good and the secret is finally out—parmesan cheese. Sometimes the polpette tasted more like parmesan than meatballs, but they were always outstanding.

Preparation time 5 minutes
Cooking time 70 minutes
Serves 4

100ml (3½ oz) olive oil
1 medium onion, finely chopped
1 clove garlic, finely chopped
1.5kg (6 cups, 3 lbs) Sugo del Giardino*
500g (1 lb) lean beef mince (ground beef)
100g (3½ oz) fresh breadcrumbs
200g (7 oz) grated parmesan cheese plus extra
  for serving

1 tablespoon finely chopped flat-leaf parsley
3 eggs, lightly beaten
salt and pepper to taste
500g (1 lb) dried spaghetti**

Preheat the oven to 180°C (350°F, Gas Mark 4).

TO MAKE THE SAUCE

Heat the olive oil in a saucepan over medium heat. Add the onion and garlic and cook, stirring, for 5 minutes. Add the sugo and bring to the boil. Reduce the heat to very low, season to taste and cook for 45 minutes.

TO MAKE THE MEATBALLS

In the meantime, combine the mince, breadcrumbs, parmesan and parsley in a bowl and mix with your hands. Add the eggs and mix well, and season to taste. Roll the mixture into plum-sized balls and place on a lightly oiled oven tray (baking sheet or cookie sheet) and cook for 10–15 minutes.

When the meatballs are cooked, remove them from the oven, and add to the sauce and cook on low heat for 10 minutes.

Cook the pasta according to the packet instructions. Drain and return to the pot. Stir in 2 ladles of the sauce with meatballs then divide the pasta among the plates, add some more sauce and top with some freshly grated parmesan cheese.

* See Basics.
** Our recipe lists dried pasta as the ingredient but you can substitute homemade or store-bought fresh pasta available from gourmet food stores and selected grocers.

BAKED PASTA WITH BEEF
Tagliatelle al forno con carne di manzo

Preparation time 15 minutes
Cooking time 70 minutes
Serves 6

100ml (3½ fl oz) olive oil
1 medium onion, chopped
2 cloves garlic, crushed
500g (1 lb) beef mince
¾ cup red cooking wine
960g (4 cups, 34 oz) Sugo del Giardino*
100g (3½ oz) mild salami, cut into small pieces
2 hard-boiled eggs, roughly chopped
500g (1 lb) fresh tagliatelle**
50g (1¾ oz) grated parmesan cheese plus
  extra to serve

100g (3½ oz) shredded mozzarella cheese
salt and pepper to taste plus an extra good
  pinch of salt to cook the pasta

TO MAKE THE SAUCE

Heat the olive oil in a medium-sized saucepan over medium heat. Add the onion and garlic and cook, stirring occasionally, until browned. Add the beef mince and stir to cook until the liquid evaporates. Add the red wine and simmer for 5 minutes. Add the Sugo and simmer on low heat for 10–20 minutes. Season to taste. Stir in the salami and eggs, and remove from the heat.

TO PREPARE THE PASTA

Fill a large saucepan with water and bring to the boil. Add a good pinch of salt to the pasta, and cook until al dente. Remove from heat and drain, then return the pasta to the saucepan and stir in three-quarters of the cooked sauce to the pasta.

TO ASSEMBLE THE PASTA BAKE

Preheat the oven to 180°C (350°F, Gas Mark 4).

In a baking dish, pour a layer of the sauce onto the base. Add the pasta–sauce combination. Top with the remaining sauce. Sprinkle with parmesan and mozzarella. Cover the dish with foil and bake in the oven for approximately 30 minutes, or until the cheese has browned.

Serve topped with freshly grated parmesan cheese.

* See Basics.
** Our recipe lists fresh pasta as the ingredient, which you can buy from selected gourmet food stores and selected grocers. You can substitute with dried pasta but we have not tested it with this recipe.

Pasta, Risotto and Pizza

VEGETABLE LASAGNA

Lasagna verdura

Preparation time 30 minutes
Cooking time 50 minutes
Serves 8

4 red capsicums (sweet or bell peppers), seeds
   and core removed and sliced
2 large Spanish onions, sliced ½ cm (¼ in)
   thick
2 tablespoons olive oil
salt and pepper to taste
1.5kg (3 lb) butternut pumpkin, sliced ½ cm
   (¼ in) thick
1kg (2 lb) Sugo del Giardino*

400g (13 oz) fresh lasagna sheets (lasagna
   noodles)**
3 zucchini (courgettes), sliced ½ cm (¼ in)
   thick
200g (7 oz) freshly grated parmesan cheese
450g (2 cups, 1 lb) shredded mozzarella
   cheese
100g (3½ oz) baby spinach

Preheat the oven to 180°C (350°F, Gas Mark 4).

Combine the capsicum and onions in a bowl, drizzle with the olive oil and season to taste. Spread onto a flat tray and roast for 20 minutes, or until soft.

Lay the pumpkin slices on a separate tray and roast for 12–15 minutes, until al dente.

Spread a full ladle of Sugo into a greased deep baking tray. Cover the Sugo with lasagna sheets (lasagna noodles) and then spread another ladle of Sugo on top. Cover with the zucchini (courgettes) and sprinkle with 20g (1 tablespoon) parmesan and 100g (3½ oz) of mozzarella.

Place another layer of lasagna sheets on top, and spread another ladle full of Sugo over that. Cover with three-quarters of the pumpkin, and sprinkle with 20g (1 tablespoon) of the parmesan and 100g (3½ oz) of the mozzarella.

Place another layer of lasagna sheets on top and spread another ladle full of Sugo on top. Cover with ¾ of the capsicum–onion mix and the spinach, and sprinkle with 20g (1 tablespoon) of the parmesan and 100g (3½ oz) of the mozzarella.

Place a final layer of lasagna sheets on top and spread 250g (1 cup, 8 oz) Sugo on top, ensuring the lasagna sheets are well covered with the sauce.

Top with the remaining pumpkin, capsicum mix and cheeses.

Bake for 45 minutes until golden brown and cooked through. Rest for 15 minutes before serving.

* See Basics.
** Our recipe lists fresh lasagna sheets as the ingredient, which you can buy at selected gourmet food stores or selected grocers. You can substitute dried sheets and prepare according to the pack instructions.

> "On a cool winter's evening in Balmain, two charming Mediterranean gentlemen ushered two sassy sisters into a renovation catastrophe to sample what has become an icon, great Bertoni coffee. Over the last five years, Bertoni has taken family tradition, family values and family cooking to the streets…We are so proud of them. "
>
> *Georgina & Jacqueline*

SPINACH AND RICOTTA CANNELLONI
Cannelloni di ricotta e spinaci

This dish is one of Bertoni's most popular.

Preparation time 25 minutes
Cooking time 30 minutes
Serves 8

1kg (2 lb) fresh ricotta cheese
250g (8 oz) spinach, blanched and chopped
90g (3 oz) freshly grated parmesan cheese plus
  extra for serving
¼ teaspoon ground nutmeg
salt and pepper to taste
325ml (1¼ cups, 11 fl oz) vegetable stock
27 dried cannelloni tubes*
480g (2 cups, 1 lb) Sugo del Giardino**
150g (5 oz) shredded mozzarella cheese

Place ricotta, spinach, 50g (1¾ oz) parmesan and the nutmeg into a food processor and season with salt and pepper. Process until smooth and set aside.

Preheat the oven to 180°C (350°F, Gas Mark 4).

Place the vegetable stock into a medium-sized saucepan over medium heat and bring to the boil. Reduce the heat to very low and maintain a simmer.

Spread 330g (11 oz) of the Sugo into a large, greased baking dish. Pipe the ricotta mix into the tubes using a piping bag and lay them flat in the baking dish. Cover the cannelloni with the hot vegetable stock and sprinkle with the remaining parmesan and the mozzarella. Bake for 30 minutes or until the cheese is golden.

Heat the remaining Sugo in a saucepan over medium heat for 5–15 minutes, stirring occasionally, until the desired thickness of sauce is reached. Put the cannelloni on plates and serve topped with the remaining Sugo and parmesan cheese.

* Our recipe lists dried pasta as the ingredient but you can substitute homemade or store-bought fresh pasta available from gourmet food stores and selected grocers.
** See Basics.

BERTONI'S TRADITIONAL BEEF LASAGNA
Lasagna alla Bertoni

We vote this the best lasagna recipe in the world. The meat sauce is thick and the bechamel is creamy. The taste—'fawghet about it'!

Preparation time 30 minutes
Cooking time 2.5 hours
Serves 8–10

MEAT SAUCE
1 brown onion, roughly chopped
2 carrots, roughly chopped
2 stalks celery, roughly chopped
¼ bunch basil leaves
3 tablespoons olive oil
1kg (2 lb) beef mince
140g (5 oz) tomato paste (tomato puree)
500ml (2 cups, 17 fl oz) vegetable stock
200ml (7 fl oz) red wine
1.4kg (6 cups, 3 lb) Sugo del Giardino*
salt and pepper to taste

BECHAMEL SAUCE
850ml (3½ cups, 30 fl oz) milk
60g (2 oz) butter
60g (2 oz) plain flour (all-purpose flour)
small pinch ground nutmeg
salt and white pepper to taste

LASAGNA ASSEMBLY
400g (13 oz) fresh lasagna sheets (lasagna noodles)**
150g (5 oz) freshly grated parmesan cheese
520g (1 lb 2 oz) shredded mozzarella cheese
1 tablespoon dried oregano leaves

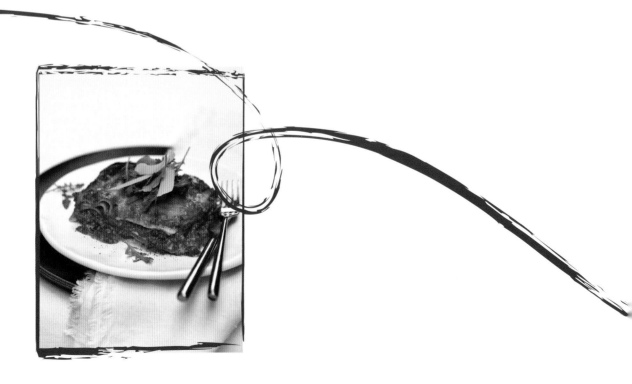

To make the meat sauce

Process the onion, carrots, celery and basil in a food processor until puréed. Heat the oil in a large, heavy-based saucepan over medium heat, add the vegetables and sauté for 5–7 minutes. Add the mince, breaking it up with your fingers as you add it to the pot to prevent large clumps of mince in the sauce, and cook until the meat is browned, stirring occasionally to keep breaking up the mince. Add the tomato paste and stir continuously for 5 minutes. Add the vegetable stock, red wine and Sugo and bring to the boil. Then reduce the heat to low and simmer for 1 hour, stirring occasionally. Season to taste, and then simmer for another 30 minutes or until the sauce has thickened.

To make the bechamel sauce

Pour the milk into a medium-sized saucepan and bring to the boil over medium heat. Remove from the heat and set aside, but keep the milk hot.

To make the roux, melt the butter in a frying pan on medium heat and stir in the flour until it is incorporated and free of lumps. Cook for 5–8 minutes until a creamy sandy texture has developed. Carefully pour the milk into the roux mixture, whisking as you pour, and continue to whisk until the sauce is thickened. Reduce the heat to low, add the nutmeg and season to taste, whisking it in until well incorporated. Allow the bechamel to slowly come to the boil. Once a few bubbles have surfaced, remove the saucepan from the heat and put a piece of plastic wrap on the surface of the sauce to prevent a skin forming. Set aside to cool.

To assemble the lasagna

Preheat oven to 180°C (350°F, Gas Mark 4).

Mix 2 heaped ladles of cooled bechamel into the meat sauce. Spread a small amount of the meat sauce onto the base of a greased, deep baking dish. Cover with a layer of lasagna sheets. Top with more meat sauce. Sprinkle with 20g of the parmesan (1 tablespoon) and 100g (3½ oz) of the mozzarella.

Repeat this process with 4 additional layers of lasagna sheets, ensuring the pasta sheets are well covered with sauce each time, and the tray is quite full. Spread remaining bechamel on top layer and sprinkle with the dried oregano leaves and bake for approximately 40 minutes until pasta is cooked and golden brown.

Set aside to rest for 15 minutes before serving.

Note: The meat sauce can be made a day in advance. After cooking, allow to cool and then cover and refrigerate.
* See Basics.
** Our recipe lists fresh lasagna sheets as the ingredient, which you can buy in gourmet food stores and selected grocers. You can substitute dried sheets and prepare according to the pack instructions.

SPICY PASTA

Pasta puttanesca

You want to put dinner on the table in just 15 minutes? Well, this recipe is about as simple as it gets, as the sauce we've listed is store-bought. Puttanesca is a spicy, salty sauce made with lots of fresh chillies, capers and olives so this simple dish is great if you like your pasta with a bit of a bite. We make our pasta puttanesca with malfalde, which is a wide flat pasta with ruffled edges, as the thickness and texture of this pasta complements the thick spicy sauce. But if you want to mix it up a bit, you can substitute a pasta of your choice.

Preparation time 1 minute
Cooking time 15 minutes
Serves 4

good pinch of salt to cook the pasta
500g (1 lb) dried malfalde pasta*
250g (1 cup, 8 oz) puttanesca sauce**
   (store-bought)
freshly grated parmesan to serve

Add salt to 5 litres of boiling water and cook the pasta according to the packet instructions. Drain the pasta and then return it to the pot.

   Heat the puttanesca sauce over a low heat in a medium-sized frying pan.

   Add 90 per cent of the puttanesca sauce to the pasta and stir to combine. Serve topped with the remaining sauce and freshly grated parmesan.

Note. If you want to lighten the spicy flavour you can mix the puttanesca with some Sugo del Giardino, to your taste.
* Our recipe lists dried pasta as the ingredient but you can substitute homemade or store-bought fresh pasta available from gourmet food stores and selected grocers.
** See Basics.

RAVIOLI IN PUMPKIN SAGE SAUCE
Ravioli con salsa di zucca e salvia

We've listed fresh store-bought ravioli for this recipe for ease of preparation but if you prefer to make your own ravioli from scratch "alla Bertoni", we've included the recipe for that too. Once you have your dough, it's easy to prepare the pasta for cooking and you can prepare the ravioli up to 6 hours ahead of time.

Preparation time 10 minutes
Cooking time 45 minutes
Serves 4

2 tablespoons olive oil
650g (23 oz) butternut pumpkin, roughly chopped
1 brown onion, roughly chopped
2 stalks celery, roughly chopped
3 tablespoons finely chopped flat-leaf parsley
3 tablespoons finely chopped sage
15ml (3 teaspoons) brandy
400ml (1¾ cups, 14 fl oz) vegetable stock
salt and pepper to taste, plus an extra good pinch of salt to cook the pasta
625g (22 oz) fresh spinach and ricotta ravioli (store-bought or see the recipe)

100g (3½ oz) baby spinach, washed and drained
parmesan cheese to serve

SPINACH AND RICOTTA RAVIOLI
60g (¼ cup, 2 oz) baby spinach leaves, shredded
500g (1 lb) low-fat ricotta cheese
500g (1 lb) plain flour (all-purpose flour)
4 eggs, plus 1 lightly beaten egg for brushing
salt and pepper to taste

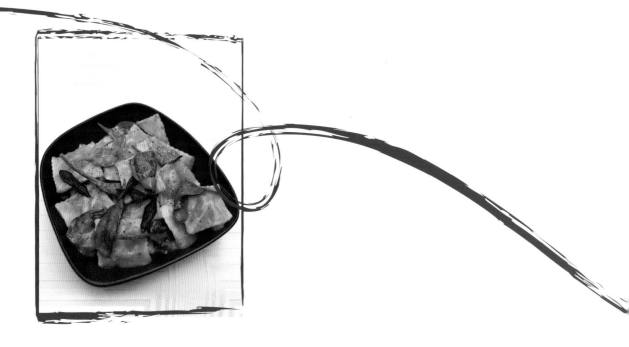

Heat the oil in a frying pan and sauté the pumpkin, onion and celery for about 5 minutes or until softened. Add the parsley, sage, brandy and stock, and bring to the boil. Reduce the heat and simmer for 30 minutes. Once the vegetables are very soft, remove from the heat and process in a blender or stick blender until smooth. Season to taste.

If you are using store-bought ravioli, cook it according to the packet instructions. If you are cooking your own ravioli, cook in batches in salted boiling water for about 4 minutes until al dente.

Drain the pasta and then return it to the pot. Add 90 per cent of the pumpkin sauce and the spinach leaves and stir to combine.

Serve topped with the remaining sauce and freshly grated parmesan cheese.

To make your own spinach and ricotta ravioli

Combine the spinach and ricotta cheese in a bowl and season to taste. Set aside.

In the meantime, place the flour in a large bowl. Make a well in the centre and add the eggs, breaking them up with a fork as you add them. Mix with your hands to incorporate the flour to make a dough, then put the dough on a floured surface and knead until it is smooth, silky and elastic. Cover with plastic wrap and rest in the refrigerator for about 30 minutes. Your dough is now ready to use.

Divide the dough into 3–4 portions. Use a rolling pin to roll them out one by one on a well-floured surface (keeping the remaining portions covered until you are ready to roll them out) until the dough is about 1.5 mm ($\frac{1}{20}$ in) thick and smooth in texture.

Working with one sheet at a time (keeping the others covered), cut into 6 cm (2½ in) squares. Place a teaspoon of the spinach–ricotta mixture in the centre of half the squares. Dip a pastry brush into the beaten egg and brush the pasta around the edge. Then carefully lay a plain square over the top of each one. Press firmly to seal the edges. Repeat with the remaining sheets.

Your ravioli are now ready to cook or you can keep them refrigerated on a floured tray for up to 4 hours.

Note: Instead of hand-kneading, you can use a pasta machine to roll out the dough. Start with the widest setting and reduce the setting as you go until you reach the required thickness.

PASTA WITH EGGPLANT FINGERS IN SUGO
Melanzane a fuchetti

As an alternative to parmesan cheese, you can top this dish with ricotta salata which will give the dish a salty and concentrated ricotta flavour. Ricotta salata is a firm cheese made from fresh ricotta that is pressed, salted and sun-dried.

Preparation time 15 minutes
Cooking time 40 minutes
Serves 4

1 kg (2 lb) eggplant (aubergine)
good pinch of salt
240ml (1 cup, 8 fl oz) oil for deep frying
   (vegetable or cottonseed oil)
500g (1 lb) pasta of your choice (dried or fresh)
60ml (¼ cup, 2 fl oz) olive oil
3 cloves garlic, finely chopped

300g (10 oz) very-ripe tomatoes, roughly
   chopped
500g (1 lb) Sugo del Giardano*
4 stalks basil, leaves only
grated parmesan cheese or ricotta salata, to
   serve

Wash the eggplant (aubergine) and slice it into 1 cm (½ in) fingers. Place the sliced eggplant in a colander and sprinkle all pieces generously with salt. Leave to stand in the colander under a weight (like a heavy plate or bowl of water) for up to 1 hour to extract the bitter juices. Rinse well under cold water and pat dry with paper towels.

Heat the vegetable oil in a frying pan to 180°C (350°F). You can test the oil by sprinkling a touch of flour into the centre. If the flour floats, the oil is ready. Fry the eggplant fingers in batches until cooked and golden brown. Drain on paper towels.

Note. At this stage you can use the eggplant fingers as they are as an antipasto dish or continue the recipe below to make the pasta dish.

In a separate pot, cook the pasta according to the packet instructions. Drain well and return the pasta to the pot.

Discard the oil used for deep frying, and heat 60ml (¼ cup, 2 fl oz) olive oil in the same frying pan over medium heat. Cook the garlic until golden brown. Add the tomatoes and cook for 15 minutes, stirring occasionally. Add the eggplant fingers and cook for a further 15 minutes. Stir through the whole basil leaves and remove from heat.

Stir the sauce through the cooked pasta, and top with a generous sprinkle of grated parmesan or ricotta salata.
   * See Basics.

STUFFED PASTA SHELLS

Conchiglie ripieni

This dish is also a great way to use up leftover vegetables so you can substitute the zucchini with whatever vegetables you have in the fridge.

Preparation time 40 minutes
Cooking time 45 minutes
Serves 4

250g (8 oz) large dried pasta shells*
2 tablespoons (¹⁄₈ cup, 1 fl oz) olive oil
700g (25 fl oz) Sugo del Giardino**
500ml (2 cups, 17 fl oz) chicken stock
250g (8 oz) grated mozzarella cheese
80g (7 tablespoons, 3 oz) grated parmesan
   cheese

CHICKEN–RICOTTA MIX
3 tablespoons olive oil
1 brown onion, finely diced
½ zucchini (courgette), grated

1 clove garlic, crushed
600g (1 lb 6 oz) chicken mince (ground
   chicken)
½ teaspoon allspice
salt and pepper to taste plus a good pinch of
   salt to cook the pasta
4 tablespoons finely chopped flat-leaf parsley
4 tablespoons finely chopped basil leaves
50g (1¾ oz) grated parmesan cheese
grated zest of 1 lemon
250g (8 oz) full cream ricotta cheese

Cook the pasta shells in boiling water with a good pinch of salt for 6 minutes only. Drain and toss through olive oil, ensuring all the shells have been separated.

Combine the Sugo and stock and set aside.

TO MAKE THE CHICKEN–RICOTTA MIX
Heat the olive oil in a frying pan over medium heat, and sauté the onion and zucchini for about 4 minutes. Add the garlic and sauté for 2 minutes, or until fragrant. Add the chicken mince, allspice, season to taste and fry continuously for 10 minutes, taking care to break up the mince to avoid large clumps. Add the parsley and basil, and cook for a further 5 minutes.

Remove from the heat and allow the mixture to cool slightly, and then fold in the parmesan, lemon zest and ricotta. Set aside.

Preheat the oven to 180°C (350°F, Gas Mark 4).

Fill each shell with a tablespoon of chicken–ricotta mix. Then place each shell neatly in a greased baking dish. Carefully pour over the combined stock and sugo, then top with the cheeses and bake for 45 minutes or until lightly golden.

Rest for 10 minutes before serving.

* Our recipe lists dried pasta as the ingredient but you can substitute homemade or store-bought fresh pasta available from gourmet food stores and selected grocers.
** See Basics.

MUSHROOM RISOTTO

Risotto ai funghi

For all the risotto recipes in this book, we recommend you use carnaroli rice, which is an Italian short-grain that has a creamy texture when cooked. This rice is considered by many Italian chefs to be the best choice for risottos. But if you can't get the carnaroli, you can substitute arborio rice.

Preparation time 10 minutes
Cooking time 40 minutes
Serves 4

1L (4 cups, 34 fl oz) vegetable stock
40g (1 oz) dried sliced porcini mushroom
50ml (1/5 cup, 1 3/4 fl oz) olive oil
40g (1 oz) butter plus 40g (1 oz) extra
1 brown onion, diced
1/4 bunch thyme, chopped

1 clove garlic, crushed
300g (10 oz) button mushrooms, quartered
260g (9 oz) carnaroli rice
100ml (1/2 cup, 4 fl oz) white wine
25ml (1 1/4 tablespoons, 3/4 fl oz) truffle oil
80g (7 tablespoons, 3 oz) parmesan cheese

Bring the stock to boil over medium heat and then reduce the heat to very low and maintain a soft simmer.

Put the porcini mushrooms in a bowl and cover with 120ml (1/2 cup, 4 fl oz) of the hot stock. Cover and soak for 20 minutes.

In the meantime, heat the olive oil and butter on a low heat in a heavy-based saucepan. Sauté the onion and thyme for 4 minutes until the onion is softened and transparent. Add the garlic and sauté for a further 2 minutes until fragrant. Drain the porcini mushrooms and retain the liquid. Add the button mushrooms to the onion—thyme mix and cook for a further 5 minutes.

Reduce the heat to low, add the rice and cook, stirring, for 5 minutes. Add the wine and allow to simmer until nearly all the wine has been absorbed, then add the porcini liquid. Once the liquid has been almost absorbed, add one ladleful of hot stock and stir to combine, and allow it to be almost absorbed before adding another ladleful. Repeat the process until the rice is al dente, reserving 120ml (1/2 cup, 4 fl oz) of the stock. Stir occasionally to avoid the rice sticking to the base of the pot and ensure all the rice grains are pushed down into the liquid once you have stirred it.

Stir in the extra butter, truffle oil and parmesan. Pour the remaining stock over the risotto, cover and set aside to rest for a few minutes before serving.

CHICKEN RISOTTO

Risotto di pollo

Preparation time 10 minutes
Cooking time 40 minutes
Serves 4

75ml (⅓ cup, 2½ fl oz) olive oil
400g (13 oz) chicken breast fillets
1L (4 cups, 34 fl oz) chicken stock
80g (3 oz) butter
1 medium brown onion, finely diced
1 clove garlic, crushed
260g (9 oz) carnaroli rice
100ml (½ cup, 3½ fl oz) white wine

60g (2 oz) basil pesto (see page 187)
60g (2 oz) baby rocket leaves
80g (7 tablespoons, 3 oz) grated parmesan
  cheese

Preheat the oven to 180°C (350°F, Gas Mark 4).

Heat 25ml (1¼ tablespoons, ¾ fl oz) of the oil in a frying pan over high heat. Season the chicken to taste and then fry it to seal until outer areas of chicken look white. Remove the chicken from heat and put it onto a baking tray (baking sheet or cookie sheet) and cook in the oven for about 10 minutes. Cover loosely with foil and set it aside to rest.

Bring the stock to boil over medium heat and then reduce the heat to very low and maintain a soft simmer.

In the meantime, heat the remaining oil and half the butter in a heavy-based saucepan over a low heat. Sauté the onion for 4 minutes until it is softened. Add the garlic and sauté for a further 2 minutes until fragrant. Add the rice and cook, stirring, for 5 minutes. Add the wine and allow to simmer until almost all of the wine has been absorbed. Once the liquid has been almost absorbed, add one ladle-full of hot stock and stir to combine, and allow it to be almost absorbed before adding another ladle-full. Repeat the process with the stock until the rice is al dente, reserving 120ml (½ cup, 4 fl oz) of stock. Stir occasionally to avoid the rice sticking to the base of the pot and ensure all the rice grains are pushed down into the liquid once you have stirred it.

Dice the chicken and add it to the risotto with the pesto, rocket leaves and remaining butter. Pour in the reserved stock and stir through until all the ingredients are combined. Cover and set aside to rest for a few minutes before serving.

Serve topped with freshly grated parmesan cheese.

Risotto with white asparagus, parmesan and truffle oil

Risotto alla Russo

Danny Russo is Australia's best modern-day chef specialising in Italian food—well we think so anyway. He made this dish for us one day at his place and it was just outstanding. We were lucky enough to convince him to share the recipe in our book.

Preparation time 5 minutes
Cooking time 30 minutes
Serves 4

1.5L (6 cups, 53 fl oz) vegetable stock
250g (8 oz) butter
1 onion, finely diced
1 clove garlic, chopped
400g (13 oz) carnaroli rice
1 bay leaf
1 bunch white asparagus, sliced into 2 cm
  (¾ in) lengths

150g (5 oz) grated parmesan cheese
2 tablespoons chopped flat-leaf parsley
salt and pepper to taste
truffle oil, to drizzle

Bring the stock to boil over medium heat and then reduce the heat to very low and maintain a soft simmer.

Slowly melt ¾ of the butter in a deep, heavy-based saucepan or pot over medium to low heat. Add the onion and garlic, and sauté until transparent. Add the rice and stir to coat it with the melted butter and lightly toast. Slowly add small amounts of vegetable stock, allowing the rice to absorb the stock entirely before adding more. Stir gently but continuously, using a wooden spoon to keep the grains separate. Add the bay leaf and the asparagus and cook until the rice is al dente and the right consistency (creamy).

Add the remaining butter, 100g (3½ oz) of the parmesan and the parsley, and stir through. Season to taste and serve drizzled with truffle oil and the remaining parmesan.

Bellissimo!

"When Bertoni first opened in 2004 I enjoyed an inaugural cup of coffee … as well as delicious treats served by Anthony, Albert, Perry … and the wonderful array of staff. My daughter has given birth to the beautiful Lotus and Jett since Bertoni opened and after each birth I was able to comfort, nourish and spoil her … with regular feasts from the café. Delicious pastas, risotto, lasagna and desserts—so appreciated on each occasion. My grandson, Mischa used to say when being collected from school in the afternoons 'Netti can we go to Bertoni for ciambelle please!' … Bertoni has become so popular from morning 'til night … always well worth it. Bertoni's fare, staff and ambience—all just divine."

Annetta

MARIA'S PIZZA DOUGH

Pizza imbasto alla Maria

Our Mum Maria has been making pizza at home for more than 40 years. She makes it with continental flour that has a high proportion of hard durum wheat, giving the dough more elasticity and bounce. Mastering your own pizza dough is an art form, but the flavour and crust you can get from a pizza base made from scratch is incomparable to most of the store-bought varieties. Traditional Italian pizza is relatively thin and crisp and topped with just a few simple and fresh ingredients. We've included some of our family's favourite toppings on the pages to follow.

Preparation time 5 minutes
Resting time 1–1.5 hours
Makes 4 × 25 cm (10 in) round pizza bases

1kg (2 lb) continental flour (plus extra to dust
   trays)*
50g (1¾ oz) fresh yeast
salt and pepper to taste plus extra good pinch
   of salt for the flour
20ml (1 tablespoon, ½ fl oz) olive oil plus extra
   for oiling trays

Place the flour in a large bowl. Put the yeast in a small bowl and stir in about 100ml (½ cup, 3½ fl oz) of water. Add the yeast mixture and the salt to the flour and mix to combine. Add 400ml (1 cup, 13 fl oz) more water and work the mixture with your fingers until the dough clumps loosely together.

Cover the bowl first with a clean tea towel (dish towel) and then with a heavy towel (ensuring no air can get through) and set aside in the coolest, darkest area on the kitchen bench to rest for 1–1½ hours. It should have risen to at least double its original size. Cut the dough into 4 equal portions. Keep all portions covered with a tea towel until you are ready to roll them out.

To make the pizza, preheat the oven to 220°C (485°F, Gas Mark 9).

Sprinkle a light layer of flour and spread a touch of olive oil onto a pizza tray (pizza pan). Place a portion of the dough onto the centre of the tray, and stretch and shape it with your fingers to cover the tray.

Choose your base type (see the next page) and add your choice of topping (see the following pages) by sprinkling all ingredients over the surface of the pizza base, season to taste and drizzle with 20ml (1 tablespoon, ½ fl oz) olive oil.

Bake for about 20–30 minutes until dough is cooked underneath and the toppings have melted.

* You'll find continental or '00' flour at most delicatessens and selected grocers. If you can't find it, you can substitute with equal parts plain flour (all-purpose flour) and fine semolina.

BERTONI'S FAMILY FAVOURITE PIZZA BASES AND TOPPINGS

Condimenti per le pizze

Base types

POMODORO (TOMATO BASE PIZZA)
Spread a generous layer of Sugo del Giardino* on the base of the pizza before adding the topping.

BIANCA (WHITE BASE PIZZA)
Add the topping directly to prepared pizza base.

PASTICCIO (PIZZA PIE)
Add ¾ of your toppings directly to the base, then add another layer of pizza base on top, pressing down to seal the sides. Top the second base with the remaining ingredients.

Toppings

MARGHERITA (TOMATO & BASIL)
150g (5 oz) very ripe tomatoes, chopped
handful of parmesan cheese, grated
1 clove garlic, chopped
100g (3½ oz) fresh buffalo mozzarella cheese or bocconcini, shredded
fresh basil leaves

PATATE (POTATO)
200g (7 oz) pontiac potatoes, thinly sliced
fresh rosemary leaves
10 black olives, pitted
handful of grated parmesan cheese
100g (3½ oz) fresh buffalo mozzarella cheese or bocconcini, shredded

MELANZANA (EGGPLANT)
200g (7 oz) eggplant (aubergine), sliced into 1 cm ($^3/_8$ in) fingers
handful of parmesan cheese, grated
100g (3½ oz) fresh buffalo mozzarella cheese or bocconcini, shredded
Prepare the eggplant by placing the slices in a colander and sprinkle all pieces generously with salt. Leave to stand in the colander under a weight (like a heavy plate or bowl of water) for 30 minutes. Rinse well under cold water and pat dry with paper towels. Then lightly fry in batches until almost cooked.

CAPSICO (CAPSICUM)
100g (3½ oz) red capsicum, sliced into 1 cm (³/₈ in) fingers
100g (3½ oz) well-ripened tomatoes, roughly chopped
handful of parmesan cheese, grated
100g (3½ oz) fresh buffalo mozzarella or bocconcini, shredded

PROSCIUTTO E RUGOLA (PROSCIUTTO & ROCKET)
60g (2 oz) ricotta cheese
4 thin slices prosciutto
handful of fresh rocket

POMODORI E OLIVE (TOMATOES & OLIVES)
20 black olives, pitted and diced
150g (5 oz) very ripe tomatoes, chopped
1 clove garlic, chopped
100g (3½ oz) fresh buffalo mozzarella or bocconcini, shredded
handful fresh basil leaves

PIZZA AL MAMMA (MAMMA'S POTATO PIZZA)
200g (7 oz) pontiac potatoes, thinly sliced
1 onion, thinly sliced
10 black olives
8 sardines, drained
scatter of fresh rosemary
handful of parmesan cheese, grated
1 well-ripened tomato, chopped roughly
salt, pepper and dried chilli flakes to taste

DOLCI (DESSERT PIZZA)
Add heaped spoonfuls of Nutella straight from the jar (as thick as you like it), and top with a good sprinkling of icing sugar

* See Basics.

Prosciutto and Rocket (page 61)
(Prosciutto e Rugola)

ZIA ROSA'S FOCCACCIA-STYLE PIZZA
Pizza siciliana come quello di Rosa

Our beloved Zia Rosa passed away in August 2009 at age 83. She was one of Dad's older sisters and a real character. She was an independent widow, living on her own right up until her passing. She didn't cook a lot, but there were a few things that she made all the time—her homemade sugo and her Pizza Siciliana. Her pizza bases were more like foccaccia and whenever she made pizza there were always two batches—a pizza to eat with her and one for us to take home. The following recipe was Zia's speciality.

Preparation time 10 minutes, resting time 3.5 hours
Makes 2 x 35 cm × 25 cm (14 ×10 in) rectangle base

PIZZA BASE
1kg (2 lb) continental flour*
50g (1¾ oz) fresh yeast
20ml olive oil
pinch of salt

TOPPING
150g Sugo del Giardino**

150g (5 oz) of mozzarella cheese or
   bocconcini, shredded
200g (7 oz) very ripe tomatoes, roughly
   chopped
2 cloves garlic, finely chopped
8 pitted black olives
8 whole anchovy fillets

Place the flour into a large bowl. Put the yeast in a small bowl and stir in about 100ml (½ cup, 3½ fl oz) of the water. Add the yeast mixture and the salt to the flour and mix to combine. Add 400ml (1 cup, 13 fl oz) more water and work with your fingers until the dough clumps together loosely.

Place the dough into a clean, lightly oiled bowl (to prevent it from sticking). Cover the bowl with a clean damp tea towel (dish towel) and then with a heavy towel (ensuring no air can get through) and set aside in the warmest, darkest area on the kitchen bench and rest for 1–1½ hours. It should have risen to at least double its original size. Cut the dough into 4 equal portions. Keep all portions covered with a tea towel until you are ready to roll them out.

Sprinkle a light layer of flour and spread a touch of olive oil onto 2 x 35 cm × 25 cm (14 ×10 in) deep rectangular baking trays. Place the dough on the centre of each tray, and stretch and shape it with your fingers to cover the base.

Place a clean damp tea towel (dish towel) securely over each tray and then top it with a heavy towel and leave to rest for an additional 30 minutes to 1 hour.

To make the pizza, preheat the oven to 220°C (420°F, Gas Mark 7).

Spread a generous layer of Sugo on the base of the pizza and scatter the mozzarella or bocconcini over the surface. Finally, sprinkle over the tomatoes, garlic, olives and whole anchovy fillets.

Bake for 30 minutes until cooked underneath and golden brown on top.

*You'll find continental or '00' flour at most delicatessens and selected grocers. If you can't find it, you can substitute with equal parts plain flour (all-purpose flour) and fine semolina.
** See Basics.

MEAT

Carne

Mum has always used many types and cuts of meat in her cooking and no matter what the meat was, she always turned it into something amazing.

Dad would often take us for a drive to the farms in the south-west of Sydney to buy fresh chickens. Within minutes of returning home, our kitchen turned into a chicken de-feathering and gutting factory. Mum would clean, prepare and freeze more than 40 chickens for family consumption over the next couple of months. And only someone who has experienced this production would be familiar with the smell that these chicken-gutting sessions would emit.

Sometimes, throughout the early 1970s, we also bought our chickens from Paddy's Markets in Haymarket. We travelled with Mum by train from Bardwell Park and our first stop would always be the 'tenor' delicatessen man who would sing Neapolitan favourites while preparing our order of Parmigiano Reggiano, mortadella, Calabrese salami, double smoked ham, prosciutto, pancetta and olives.

We would then head to the south end of the markets to visit the Chinese poultry man and Mum would select the hens directly from the cages and the poultry man would pull their necks until they snapped. While the hens were still moving, they were put into a hessian sack, which was then tied with string. That night when we ate chicken and we all decided that the taste of the freshly cooked hen outweighed the trauma we had suffered on the market trip. Sitting next to a warm bag of dead chickens, travelling the East Hills line back to our house, felt kind of normal to me.

GRILLED ITALIAN MEATBALLS

Polpette grigliata

You can serve these meatballs alone, with a side salad or dipping sauce. For a super-easy and traditional dipping sauce simply heat some Sugo del Giardano (see Basics) in a pot and serve with the warm meatballs. Another dipping sauce alternative is a basil aïoli (see page 184 for base recipe and add a few tablespoons of finely chopped basil).

Preparation time 20 minutes plus standing time
Cooking time 15 minutes
Serves 6

50g (1¾ oz) fresh breadcrumbs
50g (1¾ oz) grated parmesan cheese
handful chopped flat-leaf parsley
300g (10 oz) beef mince (ground beef)
salt and pepper to taste
1 egg
butter, for grilling

Preheat the grill (broiler).

Combine the breadcrumbs, cheese and parsley in a large bowl. Add the mince and mix with your fingers to combine, then season to taste. Add the egg and continue mixing until all the ingredients are combined and the mixture is moist. Roll mixture into balls and flatten each one a little to approximately 7 cm (2¾ in) in diameter. Refrigerate for 20 minutes.

Place the balls under a preheated grill and put a drop of butter on the top of each ball. Grill for about 6–9 minutes until browned and cooked. Turn the balls and add a drop of butter on the top of each. Grill until the other side is also browned and cooked.

Serve warm with a side salad or dipping sauce.

LAMB RISSOLES

Polpette di agnello

Preparation time 10 minutes plus standing time
Cooking time 25 minutes
Makes approximately 10 rissoles

5 tablespoons olive oil
½ Spanish onion, finely diced
1 kg (2 lb) lamb mince (ground lamb)
¼ cup finely chopped flat-leaf parsley
1 tablespoon finely chopped mint
1 tablespoon finely chopped oregano leaves
1 tablespoon finely chopped rosemary leaves

2 tablespoons fresh breadcrumbs
4 tablespoons grated parmesan cheese
1 egg
salt and pepper to taste

Preheat the oven to 200°C (400°F, Gas Mark 6).

Heat 2 tablespoons of the oil in a frying pan and sauté the onions for 4–5 minutes over medium heat. Set aside to cool.

When the onion mixture is cool, combine it with all the remaining ingredients (except the rest of the oil), in a large bowl, season to taste and mix well. Take a small amount of mixture and shape it into a patty about 8 cm (3 in) in diameter, and repeat until all the mixture has been used. Place patties on a flat tray (baking sheet or cookie sheet) lined with baking paper and refrigerate for 20 minutes.

Heat the remaining oil in a frying pan over high heat and add the rissoles in batches, and cook for about 3–4 minutes on each side, until they are browned. Remove the rissoles from heat, put them on a lined baking tray (baking sheet or cookie sheet) and bake in the oven for about 10 minutes (for medium-rare).

Serve with a leafy salad.

Beef involtini

Involtini di manzo

This dish can be prepared up to 6 hours ahead
Preparation time 20 minutes plus standing time
Cooking time 10 minutes
Serves 4

500g (1 lb) beef rump steak, cut across the
   grain into slices, 1 cm (³/₈ in) thick
70g (2½ oz) fine fresh breadcrumbs
¼ cup coarsely chopped flat-leaf parsley
1 clove garlic, finely chopped
salt and pepper to taste
200ml (7 fl oz) olive oil

12 fresh bay leaves
6 wooden skewers, pre-soaked in warm water
   for 15 minutes
lemon wedges, to serve

Lay a slice of beef between two pieces of plastic wrap and beat with a meat mallet until the meat is less than half its original thickness. Repeat with the remaining beef slices.

Combine the breadcrumbs, parsley and garlic in a bowl and season to taste. Pour 125ml (½ cup, 4 fl oz) of the olive oil into a separate shallow bowl. Dip each slice of beef into the olive oil, then coat it in the breadcrumb mixture and roll it up.

Skewer a beef roll horizontally and then follow with a bay leaf on top. Repeat with another beef roll and bay leaf. Repeat with all the beef slices. Lay the finished skewers on a tray, cover with plastic wrap and refrigerate for at least 30 minutes.

Heat the remaining oil in a large frying pan over a medium heat. Cook the involtini, in batches, turning regularly until just cooked through.

Serve immediately with some fresh lemon wedges.

"*The food at Bertoni is SIMPLY THE BEST. Ideal for people who work shift work (odd hours) like me. The food is always fresh & delicious. Nutritional too. Your number one fan.*"
Cath

SLOW-BRAISED LAMB SHOULDER WITH TOMATO, BEANS AND OLIVE RAGU

Agnello al' Russo

This is another one of Danny Russo's recipes that he has agreed to share with us. Our Mum makes a great classic lamb roast, but this dish is something else. The meat is so tender it just falls right off the bone.

You will need to start this recipe a day ahead.
Preparation time 15 minutes
Cooking time 5.5 hours
Serves 6

2 medium onions
2 medium carrots
1 medium leek (white part only)
2 stalks celery
10 ripe tomatoes
50ml (¹⁄₅ cup, 1 ¾ fl oz) olive oil
4 cloves garlic, crushed by hand
500ml (2 cups, 17 fl oz) white wine
2 × 2kg (4½ lb) lamb shoulder (bone in)
200ml chicken stock
150g (5 oz) fresh borlotti beans (roman or romano beans)
100g (3½ oz) cannellini beans, soaked in cold water overnight

100g (3½ oz) black olives, pitted
2 bay leaves
1 strip orange peel
6 juniper berries, crushed
½ bunch thyme
6 whole white peppercorns
100g (3½ oz) butter beans, blanched and cut into small pieces
100g (3½ oz) fresh broad beans (fava beans), blanched and peeled
½ bunch marjoram, leaves picked
salt and pepper to taste

Preheat the oven to 120°C (250°F, Gas Mark 1).

Wash the onion, carrots, leek and celery, and dice into 1 cm ($^3/_8$ in) cubes. Wash the tomatoes, remove the seeds and chop into 1 cm ($^3/_8$ in) pieces.

Heat the oil in a large, deep roasting tin over medium heat on the top of the stove (cooker). The tray should be big enough to fit the vegetables and the two lamb shoulders. Add the garlic and cook until golden brown. Then add the diced onions and cook until transparent. Add the carrots, celery and leek, and cook for approximately 5 minutes without colouring. Deglaze the pan with the white wine and reduce the liquid by three-quarters.

In the meantime, season the lamb and, in a separate pan, evenly brown both sides of the lamb until the meat is well sealed.

Place the lamb in the roasting tin with the vegetables. Add the chicken stock, tomatoes, borlotti and cannellini beans, 50g (1¾ oz) of the olives, the bay leaves, orange peel, juniper berries, thyme and peppercorns. Bring the liquid back to boil, then reduce the heat and cover with foil or a tight-fitting lid. Remove the tin from the heat and put it in the oven. Cook for 4–5 hours, or until the meat begins to fall away from the bone.

Once the lamb is cooked, carefully remove the shoulders from the roasting tin and put them on a serving dish.

Return the roasting tin to the top of the stove and, over medium heat, add the butter beans, broad beans, remaining olives and the marjoram, and reduce until the sauce thickens, then season to taste.

Pour the sauce over the lamb and serve.

BERTONI'S CLASSIC VEAL SHANKS
Osso bucco alla Bertoni

You will need to start this recipe a day ahead.
Preparation time 10 minutes
Cooking time 2.5 hrs
Serves 6

60ml (¼ cup, 2 fl oz) olive oil
6 pieces veal shank cut 5 cm (2 in) thick, from
    the hind leg and cut across the bone
1 cup plain flour (all-purpose flour) plus 1
    tablespoon extra
4 medium onions, sliced into 2 cm (¾ in) pieces
500g (2 cups, 1 lb) Sugo del Giardino*
125ml (½ cup, 4 fl oz) white wine

salt and pepper to taste
2 cups fresh borlotti beans (roman or romano
    beans), soaked in cold water overnight
1 cup flat-leaf parsley, roughly chopped
5 cloves garlic, finely chopped

Heat 25ml (1¼ tablespoons, ¾ fl oz) of the oil over high heat in a frying pan. Coat the veal shanks in the flour and add to the pan, cooking until it is sealed and browned. Remove from heat.

In a large saucepan, heat the remaining oil over medium heat and sauté the onions for about 3–4 minutes, until transparent. Add the veal shanks, Sugo, wine and season to taste. Bring to the boil then reduce the heat to low, and simmer, covered, for 90 minutes.

Remove 125ml (½ cup, 4 fl oz) of the liquid from the pot and mix it with the extra flour to combine. Then return the flour–sauce mixture to the pot and turn the veal shanks over. Drain the beans and add them to the pot with the parsley and garlic, return to the boil, then reduce the heat and simmer for a further 45–60 minutes.

Allow the osso bucco to rest for 10 minutes before serving. Serve on top of some creamy mashed potatoes.

* See Basics.

"Mum would clean, prepare and freeze more than 40 chickens for family consumption over the next couple of months."

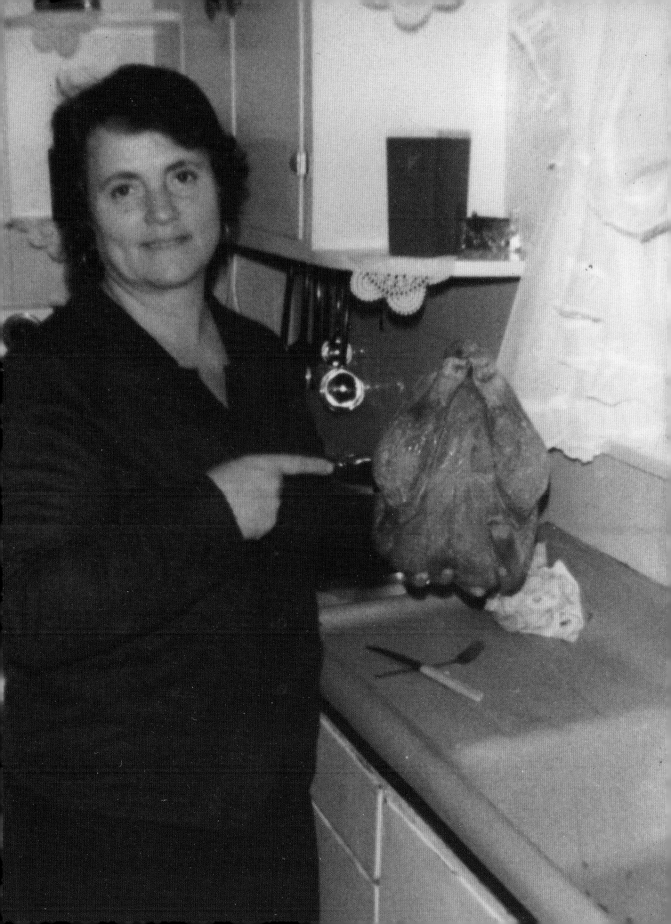

CHICKEN CACCIATORE

Pollo alla cacciatora

Preparation time 15 minutes
Cooking time 45 minutes
Serves 4

6 tablespoons olive oil
1 large onion, finely chopped
3 cloves garlic, crushed
1 stalk celery
125g (4 oz) button mushrooms, sliced
4 chicken drumsticks
4 chicken thighs
salt and pepper to taste

90ml (3 fl oz) white wine
960g (2 lb) Sugo del Giardino*
¼ teaspoon brown sugar
1 sprig oregano plus extra sprigs to garnish
1 sprig rosemary
1 bay leaf

Heat half the oil in a large casserole dish over medium heat. Add the onion, garlic and celery and cook, stirring occasionally, for about 6 minutes until the onion is golden. Increase the heat, add the mushrooms and cook for 4 minutes. Remove the mixture from the dish and set it aside.

Heat the remaining oil in the casserole dish over medium heat and lightly brown the chicken pieces in batches. Season to taste. When all the pieces have been browned, put them into the casserole dish, add the wine and cook until the liquid has evaporated.

Add the Sugo, sugar, oregano, rosemary, bay leaf and 80ml (⅓ cup, 2½ fl oz) water, and bring to the boil. Season to taste. Reduce the heat, cover the dish and simmer for 20 minutes or until the chicken is tender. Discard the cooked herbs and bay leaf, and toss in the extra sprigs of oregano to garnish.

* See Basics.

SEAFOOD

Frutti di mare

*W*hile seafood was not a central part of our diet, apart from Mum's famous garlic prawns and fried calamari, Mum had several low-budget dishes that she made occasionally. Salt-cured cod and dried stock fish (available only at old delis) were offered to us on many occasions, but we rarely ate them because we couldn't stand the strong smell. On one occasion we all revolted against the smell of the fish-stock stew and made Mum bury it in the backyard rather than make us eat it.

Summer beach trips to Botany Bay with our uncles, Zio Pepe, Giovanni and Michele, would introduce many new flavours to our family. Freshly shucked mussels, dressed with just a squeeze of lemon, were eaten direct from the rocks at Brighton Le Sands. On windy days, sea snails would wash up in the hundreds around Ramsgate, and we collected buckets-full to eat that night. Coming home one day from one of these beach trips we were all ushered out of the car on General Homes Drive to collect full beer cans from an overturned lorry: for our Dad and uncles, all immigrants from Sicily, this truly was 'the lucky country'.

SEAFOOD ANTIPASTO PLATTER

Antipasto frutti di mare

Cottonseed oil is used in this recipe mainly because it has a neutral taste so you'll get the full flavour of the seafood, but you can substitute vegetable oil.

Preparation time 20 minutes
Cooking time 20 minutes
Serves 6

1 cup flour
250g (8 oz) baby calamari (baby squid),
  cleaned and cut into 5 mm (¼ in) rings
500ml (2 cups, 17 fl oz) cottonseed oil, for
  frying
60ml (¼ cup, 2 fl oz) olive oil
250g (8 oz) baby octopus, cleaned
good quality sea salt

500g (1 lb) mussels, cleaned
4 tablespoons finely chopped parsley
grated zest of 1 lemon
crushed ice to serve
250g (8 oz) fresh, cooked prawns (shrimp)
12 fresh oysters
lemon wedges, to serve
leaf salad, to serve

Put the flour in a bowl and toss the calamari through until the pieces are evenly coated. Put the floured calamari in a sieve and shake off any excess flour. Half-fill a deep frying pan with cottonseed oil and heat to 180°C (350°F) (if the oil starts to smoke it's too hot). Add the calamari in batches and fry for about 45 seconds for each batch, or until golden brown. Drain on paper towels and season generously with sea salt.

Heat the olive oil in a frying pan over medium heat. Add the octopus and cook for about 3–5 minutes until golden brown (octopus is cooked when the tip of a knife slips through the tentacle). Drain on paper towels and season with sea salt.

Place a steamer over a medium-sized pot of simmering water. Add the mussels and steam for about 2 minutes or until the shells just open.

On one half of a large serving platter, add a row each of the calamari, octopus and mussels. Sprinkle with parsley and the grated lemon zest.

Cover the base of the remaining half of the large platter with a thin layer of crushed ice. Place the fresh prawns and oysters on the ice.

Serve the platter with lemon wedges and a leaf salad.

See picture page 86.

MARINATED ANCHOVIES

Alici marinate

This dish can be refrigerated for up to three days.

Preparation time 10 minutes plus at least 3 hours refrigeration
Serves 4

400g (13 oz) fresh anchovy fillets*
2 cloves garlic, crushed
2 tablespoons finely chopped flat-leaf parsley
2 tablespoons finely chopped basil
1 small red chilli, de-seeded and finely chopped
60ml (¼ cup, 2 fl oz) olive oil
1 tablespoon extra virgin olive oil
3 tablespoons lemon juice

salt and pepper to taste
ciabatta bread to serve

Carefully wash the anchovy fillets under cold water and pat dry with paper towels. Place the fillets in a shallow serving dish.

Mix all of the remaining ingredients to combine, season to taste and pour over the anchovy fillets. Cover with plastic wrap and refrigerate for at least 3 hours.

Serve with some fresh Italian ciabatta.

* You can substitute sardines.

GARLIC PRAWNS

Gambaretti al aglio

Preparation time 10 minutes
Cooking time 9 minutes
Serves 4

60ml (¼ cup, 2 fl oz) olive oil
80g (7 tablespoons, 3 oz) butter
½ small red chilli, finely chopped
10 cloves garlic, crushed
20 large prawns (shrimp), peeled and de-veined
60ml (¼ cup, 2 fl oz) white wine or vegetable
  stock
3 tablespoons chopped flat-leaf parsley
salt and pepper to taste

Heat the oil and butter in a large frying pan over medium heat. Add the chilli and half the garlic and cook, stirring, for about 3 minutes.

Add the prawns and the remaining garlic and cook for 3 minutes or until the prawns turn pink. Turn the prawns, add the wine or stock, and cook for a further 3 minutes.

Add parsley and season to taste. Serve hot with some fresh crusty Italian bread so your guests can mop up the garlic oil at the end.

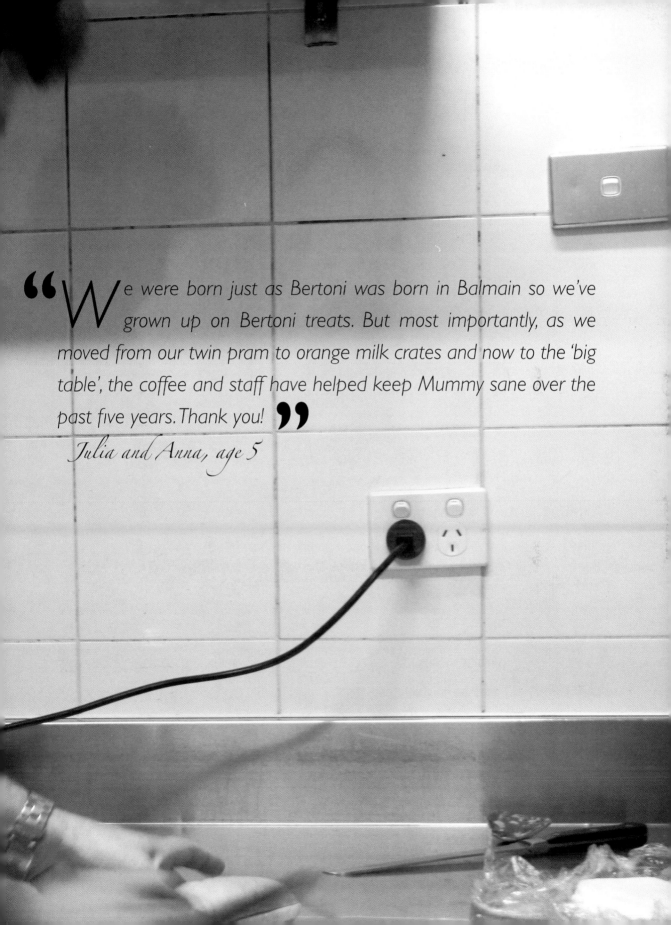

"We were born just as Bertoni was born in Balmain so we've grown up on Bertoni treats. But most importantly, as we moved from our twin pram to orange milk crates and now to the 'big table', the coffee and staff have helped keep Mummy sane over the past five years. Thank you!"

Julia and Anna, age 5

SNAPPER WRAPPED IN FENNEL AND PANCETTA
Pesce avvolto con pancetta e finocchio

Preparation time 10 minutes
Cooking time 10 minutes
Serves 4

2 x baby fennel
32 slices pancetta, very thinly sliced into long
  strips
4 × 180g (6 oz) snapper fillets, scaled and pin-
  bones removed
salt and pepper to taste
60ml (¼ cup, 2 fl oz) olive oil

Preheat the oven to 190°C (375°F, Gas Mark 5).

Blanch the baby fennel in boiling water for approximately 4 minutes. Then trim the top and tail off and separate the stalks from the bulbs. Thinly slice the bulbs lengthways and stalks in half widthways.

Lay 8 slices of pancetta on a clean work surface. The pancetta slices should be wide enough to cover each portion of fish. Place a piece of fish onto the pancetta, cover with fennel and season to taste. Carefully and tightly roll the pancetta over the fish to make a parcel, tucking the ends neatly. Refrigerate for 20 minutes.

In a medium-sized oven dish, heat the olive oil on the top of the stove (cooker) over medium heat and add the pancetta–snapper parcels. Cook for approximately 1 minute each side to seal, or until the pancetta is golden brown.

Remove the parcels from heat and then put the dish into the oven for 6–8 minutes, turning the fish after 4 minutes.

Serve immediately.

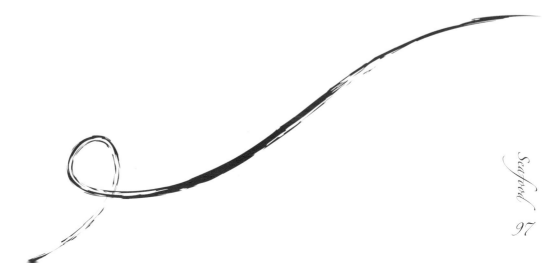

TUNA BEAN SALAD

Insalata di tonno

Preparation time 10 minutes
Cooking time 8 minutes
Serves 4 as a meal or 6 as a side

540g (19 oz) green beans
4 roma tomatoes (plum tomatoes)
½ small Spanish onion
425g (15 oz) tin tuna in oil
50g (1¾ oz) black olives
4 eggs, hard-boiled and quartered
100ml (7 fl oz) seeded mustard dressing (see
  page 188)
salt and pepper to taste

Blanch the beans in boiling water for 3 minutes, then plunge them into ice water and slice in half, on an angle. Set aside.

Cut the tomatoes into wedges. Finely slice the Spanish onion. Drain the tuna.

Place the beans, tomatoes, onion, olives, half the eggs, tuna and dressing in a large bowl and mix together and season to taste. Transfer to a shallow platter and top with the remaining quartered boiled eggs.

SOUPS AND STEWS

Zuppe e spezzatini

Soup night was once a week and Mum made a wide variety—shin beef, chicken, minestrone, white beans, broad beans, lentil, brown beans, barramundi and pork meatballs just to name a few. Dad's garden usually provided everything required for the base of the soup and Mum would always throw in a large chunk of parmesan rind. It would melt to a gooey cheese glob that we kids would always fight over.

The stews were a welcome alternative to soup when we were younger. Mum bought the meat mostly from the local butcher, but occasionally our Greek next-door neighbour would deliver a box of meat from his brother who had a farm in the Riverina region. It wasn't until years later that Mum would tell us that the 'beef' stew she used to make was often made from wild rabbit or baby goat.

The following pages offer some of the soups and stews that Mum has been making for years. Even though we serve these dishes in our cafés, Mum still makes her own batches at home, which Dad delivers to our homes almost every week. "It's good for you," Mum says. I guess she doesn't trust that we're eating enough.

FISH SOUP

Zuppa di pesce

Preparation time 20 minutes
Cooking time 70 minutes, including time to prepare the stock
Serves 6

FISH STOCK (MAKES APPROXIMATELY 1.5 LITRES OF STOCK)
300g (1⅓ cups, 10 oz) fish bones
1 small onion, roughly chopped
1 small carrot, roughly chopped
1 stalk celery, roughly chopped
2 parsley stalks
4 black peppercorns
1 bay leaf

FISH SOUP
200g (7 oz) clams
4 tablespoons olive oil plus extra for garnish
1 carrot, diced
1 stalks celery, sliced
1 baby fennel, sliced, tips reserved
2 cloves garlic, thinly sliced

small pinch cayenne pepper
1 onion, sliced
30ml (⅛ cup, 1 fl oz) Pernod
150ml (⅗ cup, 5 fl oz) white wine
700g (25 oz) Sugo del Giardino*
250g (8 oz) red mullet fillets
250g (8 oz) monkfish tails
1 squid tube, cleaned
300g (10 oz) mussels, scrubbed and de-bearded
8 scallops
200g (7 oz) cleaned baby octopus
salt and pepper to taste

To make the fish stock

Put all the ingredients in a stockpot. Pour in 2 litres of water, bring to the boil and simmer over medium heat for 20 minutes, removing scum as it rises to the surface. Strain the liquid and set aside.

To make the soup

Soak the clams in cold water until ready to use, to remove all sand and grit. Change the water if necessary to ensure the clams are thoroughly cleaned.

On a medium heat, pour the oil into a heavy-based saucepan, then add the carrots, celery, fennel, garlic, cayenne pepper and onion, and sauté for 8 minutes. Add the Pernod and simmer until evaporated, then add the white wine and simmer for 2 minutes. Add the Sugo and fish stock. Bring to the boil, reduce heat and simmer for 50 minutes.

In the meantime, prepare the fish. Cut the fish into large, fork-sized chunks. Drain the clams. Cut and score the squid in a criss-cross pattern, then cut into pieces roughly the same size as the fish pieces. Once the soup has reduced, taste for seasoning, and then add the octopus and the squid, cook for 1 minute. Then add the fish, cook for 1 minute, then add the drained clams, mussels and scallops. Cook until the mussels and clams have opened, and remove the soup from the heat.

Pour the fish and the soup into a large bowl, then drizzle some olive oil on top and garnish with the reserved fennel tips.

Serve with some grilled bread.

See Basics.

THE BEST CHICKEN SOUP EVER

Brodo di pollo

Our Mum has been making this chicken soup since we were kids and we think it's the best chicken soup ever. We're not kids any more and we are all married with our own families now, but within hours of anyone falling sick with a flu or cold, a pot of Mum's freshly made chicken soup is delivered to our door.

Preparation time 5 minutes
Cooking time 70 minutes
Serves 6–8

1 large onion
2 medium carrots
¾ bunch celery
1 medium-sized whole chicken
250g (1 cup, 8 oz) Sugo del Giardino*
200g (7 oz) frozen peas, thawed
2 tablespoons grated parmesan cheese
salt and pepper to taste

Dice the onion, carrots and celery into 1 cm (½ in) cubes and set aside.

Put 4 litres of water in a large saucepan and bring to the boil over medium heat.

Wash the chicken, remove the skin and cut the chicken into quarters.

When the water in the saucepan is boiling, add the chicken and bring to the boil again, then reduce the heat to low. Add the Sugo, all the vegetables, including the peas, and cook for 30 minutes.

Remove the chicken from the saucepan and allow it to cool slightly. Then, with your hands, shred the chicken into small pieces. Return the shredded chicken to the pot and cook for 30 minutes. Stir in the parmesan and season to taste.

Allow to rest for 10 minutes and skim any fat that has formed at the top before serving.

* See Basics.'

MINESTRONE SOUP

Zuppa di verdura

Start this recipe a day ahead.
This soup can be frozen for up to 2 months in an airtight container.

Preparation time 15 minutes
Cooking time 110 minutes
Serves 10

½ cup dried chickpeas (garbanzo beans)
½ cup dried borlotti beans (roman or romano beans)
1 tablespoon olive oil plus extra to drizzle
1 onion, finely diced
1 leek (white part only), finely chopped
1 carrot, cut into 1 cm (³/₈ in) cubes
¼ small Japanese pumpkin (about 400 g, or 13 oz) peeled, cut into 1 cm (³/₈ in) cubes
2 medium potatoes (about 200 g, or 7 oz, each), peeled, cut into 1 cm (³/₈ in) cubes

½ large kumara (sweet potato) (about 200 g, or 7 oz), peeled, cut into 1 cm (³/₈ in) cubes
2L (8 cups, 67 fl oz) vegetable stock
2 dried bay leaves
2 zucchini (courgettes), cut into 1 cm (³/₈ in) cubes
1 cup broccoli or cauliflower florets
2 oven-roasted tomatoes, finely chopped*
65g (¼ cup, 2½ oz) pesto (see page 186)
½ cup finely chopped basil leaves
salt and pepper to taste

Soak the chickpeas and borlotti beans separately in cold water for 6 hours or overnight.

Cook the chickpeas over high heat for 50 minutes and the borlotti beans for 30 minutes in separate saucepans of boiling water until tender, then drain. Cover with cold water and set aside.

Boil a pot of water (or a kettle) and set aside. Heat the oil in a large stockpot or deep saucepan over medium heat. Add the onion and leek, and cook, stirring, for 5 minutes until soft but not coloured. Add the carrot, pumpkin, potato and kumara and cook, stirring, for 5 minutes. Add the stock, bay leaves, zucchini, broccoli or cauliflower, tomatoes and 2 cups boiling water and bring to a simmer. Reduce the heat a little and simmer for 20 minutes, stirring occasionally, or until the vegetables are tender. Add the drained beans and chickpeas, with the pesto, basil and enough extra boiling water to cover the vegetables. Cook for a further 3–5 minutes or until heated through.

Season with sea salt and freshly ground black pepper and drizzle with extra olive oil to serve.

* Prepared oven-roasted tomatoes are available from supermarket deli counters or delicatessens.

BORLOTTI BEAN SOUP

Zuppa di fagioli

Start this recipe a day ahead.

Preparation time 5 minutes
Cooking time 75 minutes
Serves 4

*500g (1 lb) dried borlotti beans (roman or
   romano beans)*
1 teaspoon bicarbonate of soda (baking soda)
½ bunch celery
1 carrot
1 onion
100ml (½ cup, 3½ fl oz) olive oil
250g (1 cup, 8 oz) Sugo del Giardino*
salt and pepper to taste
ciabatta bread, to serve

Soak the beans in water and the bicarbonate of soda for 6 hours or overnight. Rinse well the next morning.

Wash and trim the celery and carrot, and peel the onion and dice them all into small cubes.

Put 3 litres of cold water into a large saucepan over high heat and bring it to the boil. Add the beans and bring to the boil again. Add the vegetables, oil and Sugo and bring to boil.

Reduce the heat to medium, season to taste and cook for approximately 1 hour or until the beans are cooked.

Serve hot with some crusty Italian ciabatta.

* See Basics.

LENTIL SOUP

Lenticchie

Start this recipe a day ahead.

Preparation time 5 minutes
Cooking time 75 minutes
Serves 4

500g (1 lb) dried brown lentils
1 teaspoon bicarbonate of soda (baking soda)
½ bunch celery
1 carrot
1 onion
100ml (½ cup, 3½ fl oz) olive oil
250g (1 cup, 8 oz) Sugo del Giardino*
salt and pepper to taste
grated parmesan cheese, to serve

Soak the lentils in water and the bicarbonate of soda for 6 hours or overnight. Rinse well the next morning.

Wash and trim the celery and carrot, peel the onion and dice them all into small cubes.

Put 3 litres of cold water into a large saucepan over high heat and bring it to the boil. Add the lentils and bring to the boil again. Add the vegetables, oil and sugo and bring to the boil.

Reduce the heat to medium, season to taste and cook for approximately 1 hour or until the lentils are soft.

Serve hot, topped with some grated parmesan cheese.

* See Basics.

Sicilian broad bean soup

Macco

Start this recipe a day ahead.

Preparation time 5 minutes
Cooking time 120 minutes
Serves 4

500g (1 lb) dried broad beans (fava beans)
1 teaspoon bicarbonate of soda (baking soda)
½ bunch celery
1 medium-sized zucchini (courgette)
1 large onion
250g (1 cup, 8 oz) Sugo del Giardino*
100g (3½ oz) tomato paste (tomato puree)
100ml (½ cup, 3½ fl oz) olive oil
salt and pepper to taste

Soak the beans in water and the bicarbonate of soda for 6 hours or overnight. Rinse well the next morning and remove the beans from their shell.

Wash and trim the celery stalks and zucchini, and peel the onion, and dice them all into small 1.5cm cubes.

Put 3 litres of cold water into a large saucepan over high heat and bring it to the boil. Add the beans and bring to the boil again and cook for approximately 20 minutes. Add the Sugo, tomato paste and oil, and season to taste. Reduce the heat and simmer for about 90 minutes, stirring occasionally, until the soup has reduced and thickened.

* See Basics.

LAMB STEW

Spezzatino di agnello

Preparation time 15 minutes
Cooking time 80 minutes
Serves 6

40ml (2 tablespoons, 1³/₅ fl oz) olive oil plus
   40ml (2 tablespoons, 1³/₅ fl oz) extra
1kg (2 lb) trimmed and diced lamb (such as
   boneless lamb shoulder or stewing lamb)
2 carrots, roughly chopped
2 stalks celery, roughly chopped
2 onions, roughly chopped
1 bay leaf
5 juniper berries
1 cup finely chopped thyme
1 cup finely chopped rosemary

1 cup finely chopped sage
60g (¼ cup, 2 oz) tomato paste
   (tomato puree)
250ml (1 cup, 8 fl oz) red wine
250g (1 cup, 8 oz) Sugo del Giardino*
400ml (1¾ cups, 14 fl oz) beef stock
salt and pepper to taste
400g (13 oz) potatoes, diced into 1 cm (1/2 in)
   pieces
200g (7 oz) button mushrooms, quartered
50ml (¹/₅ cup, 1¾ fl oz) marsala

Heat 40ml (2 tablespoons, 1³/₅ fl oz) of the oil over high heat in a heavy-based saucepan. Brown the lamb in batches then remove from saucepan and set aside.

To the same pot, add the carrot, celery, onion, bay leaf, juniper berries and the herbs, and sauté for 3 minutes. Stir in the tomato paste and cook for an additional 3 minutes, stirring occasionally. Add the lamb, and pour in the red wine, Sugo, stock and oil, and season to taste.

Reduce the heat to medium and cook for 30–40 minutes, or until the lamb is tender. Add the potatoes and mushrooms and continue cooking for about 20–30 minutes, or until the potatoes are cooked and the liquid has thickened.

Stir in the marsala and serve alone or over some cooked rice.

* See Basics.

VEGETABLES

Verdure

There was always an array of vegetables available in Dad's backyard 'family farm' and Mum knew how to make endless dishes with all of them—tomatoes, beans, zucchini (courgette), eggplant (aubergine), baby carrots, potatoes, onions, garlic, artichokes, fresh herbs and chilli.

During the school holidays, all of us kids would help Dad toil in the garden. We'd make regular trips to chicken farms and load up the car with as many bags of warm, smelly chicken manure as we could fit. When we got it home, we would have to distribute and plough it by treading ankle-deep through the chicken poo. Dad, like many of his generation, truly understood the meaning of eating an organic diet, and the manure he used to enrich his soil always came from cows or chickens. And he never believed in using commercial sprays on his fruit and vegetables—he only ever used coffee or garlic to keep the bugs at bay.

While this was happening outside, Mum was inside cooking and cleaning, but she ventured into the backyard at perfect intervals with plates of freshly filled panini, roast capsicums, still warm from the oven and dressed only with garlic and olive oil, and cold espresso coffee.

POTATO CROQUETTES

Crocchette di patate

Preparation time 10 minutes
Cooking time 30 minutes
Serves 4

1 kg (2 lb) pontiac potatoes
50g (1¾ oz) butter
200g (7 oz) grated parmesan cheese
3 sprigs flat-leaf parsley, chopped
5 eggs
salt and pepper to taste
200g (7 oz) plain flour (all-purpose flour)
250g (1 cup) fresh breadcrumbs
200ml (7 fl oz) olive oil, for frying
12 slices provolone cheese, to serve

Wash the potatoes well, leaving the skin on. Put them into a large saucepan and cover with cold water. Bring to the boil over a medium heat then reduce the temperature to low and simmer for about 15–20 minutes or until the potatoes are cooked. Drain and allow to cool for a few minutes before carefully peeling off the skin. Place the potatoes in a large bowl and mash or put through a ricer.

Add the butter, parmesan and parsley, and, using your hands, mix well to combine all the ingredients. Roll the mixture into balls about the size of a small plum and set aside.

In a shallow dish, whisk the eggs well and season with salt and pepper. Place the flour in one separate shallow dish and the breadcrumbs in another. Dip each croquette first into the flour, then the egg, and finally the breadcrumbs, ensuring the croquettes are coated well.

Heat the oil in a large frying pan over high heat and fry the croquettes in batches until golden brown, turning as required. Drain on a paper towel.

To serve, place some sliced provolone cheese onto the centre of a platter and surround it with the hot croquettes.

STUFFED ARTICHOKES

Carciofi impottiti

Preparation time 35 minutes
Cooking time 30 minutes
Serves 4

6 tender artichokes
juice of 1 lemon
3 sardines, chopped (fresh or tinned and
    drained of oil)
6 stalks flat-leaf parsley, chopped
4 cloves garlic, finely chopped
100g (3½ oz) pitted black olives, chopped
30g (1 oz) capers, rinsed

60ml (¼ cup, 2 fl oz) olive oil, plus extra to
    drizzle
salt and pepper to taste
100g (3½ oz) bread, crust removed and torn
    into small pieces
handful of fresh breadcrumbs

Preheat the oven to 180°C (350°F, Gas Mark 4).

Clean the artichokes well and soak them in water with the juice of 1 lemon for approximately 30 minutes. Rinse well and then tap each artichoke on the edge of a bench until the top opens. Set aside.

In a medium bowl, place the sardines, parsley, garlic, olives, capers and the oil, and mix well to combine all ingredients. Season to taste.

Lightly pack the mixture into each artichoke and stand them upright in a baking dish. Pack the artichokes tightly to prevent them opening any further during cooking. (You can also secure each artichoke by tying cooking string around it.)

Top each artichoke with the bread and breadcrumbs, and drizzle with a little olive oil and 1 cup lukewarm water. Bake for about 20–30 minutes until cooked.

Can be served immediately or made several hours ahead and re-heated before serving.

MAMMA'S SICILIAN VEGETABLE ANTIPASTO
Mamma's caponata

This dish can be served cold or warm and straight from the fridge or oven. It will keep in the refrigerator for up to 1 week if stored in an airtight container.

Preparation time 5 minutes
Cooking time 60 minutes
Serves 8

3 large eggplant (aubergines)
4 red capsicums (sweet or bell peppers)
4 tomatoes, very ripe
1 clove garlic
4–5 sprigs basil, chopped
1 teaspoon oregano
100ml (½ cup, 3½ fl oz) olive oil
salt and pepper to taste
parmesan cheese, to serve

crusty Italian bread or homemade crostini, to
 serve

BAKED CROUTONS
1 clove garlic, crushed
60ml (¼ cup, 2 fl oz) Olio Verde*
12 slices day-old ciabatta bread, sliced about
 1.5 cm (½ in) thick

Preheat the oven to 180°C (350°F, Gas Mark 4).

Wash the eggplant and capsicum and dry well with paper towel. Slice them into 1 cm (½ in) strips. Chop the tomatoes and the garlic, and combine them with the eggplant and capsicum in a large bowl. Add the basil leaves, oregano and oil, and season to taste.

Add ½ cup of water and mix well to combine. Place the mixture in a shallow roasting dish (roasting tin) and cook for approximately 1 hour, turning occasionally.

This dish can be served hot or cold.

Serve with some chunks of Reggiano parmesan cheese and crusty Italian bread or homemade crostini.

To make the baked croutons
Preheat the oven to 180°C (350°F, Gas Mark 4) (or preheat the grill or broiler).

Combine the oil and garlic in a small bowl and mix well. Using a pastry brush, brush both sides of the bread slices, and then bake or grill until crisp.

Remove from the oven and top with Mamma's caponata.

* See Basics.

BROAD BEAN FRITTATA

Fave verde fritte

Preparation time 5 minutes
Cooking time 30 minutes
Serves 4

6 eggs
salt and pepper to taste
100ml (½ cup, 3½ fl oz) olive oil
1 large onion, finely chopped
1kg (2lb) broad beans (fava beans), fresh or
frozen, shells removed
handful parmesan cheese, grated

Whisk the eggs in a bowl, season to taste and set aside.

Heat the oil in a large frying pan over medium heat and cook the onion for 4–5 minutes, stirring occasionally, until it is soft and brown. Add the beans and cook, stirring, for about 20 minutes or until cooked.

Add the eggs and the parmesan cheese, stirring carefully to mix the egg mixture evenly throughout the beans. Allow to set, and then flip the frittata (like a pancake) to cook the other side until golden brown.

Remove from the heat and leave to cool before cutting into wedges and serving.

Eggplant parmigiana

Parmigiana di melanzane

Start this recipe a day ahead.
Preparation time 1 hour
Cooking time 20 minutes plus resting time
Serves 4

6 eggs, lightly beaten
3 tablespoons chopped flat-leaf parsley
salt and pepper to taste
400ml (13 oz) olive oil
2kg (4 lb) eggplant (aubergine), sliced length-
*   ways ½ cm (¹/₈ in) thick*
*960g (2 lb) Sugo del Giardino**
120g (3¾ oz) freshly grated parmesan cheese
270g (9 oz) mozzarella cheese, shredded
cracked black pepper
¼ cup fresh breadcrumbs

In a small bowl, mix together the beaten eggs and parsley and season to taste.

Heat the olive oil in a frying pan over medium heat. Dip each slice of eggplant into the egg mix and fry, in batches, until tender. Drain on paper towel to remove excess oil.

Preheat the oven to 180°C (350°F, Gas Mark 4).

Spread ½ cup of the Sugo over the base of a greased lasagne dish. Top with a layer of the eggplant, using about one-quarter of the eggplant slices. Sprinkle with 20g (1 tablespoon, ½ oz) of the parmesan cheese and a handful of the mozzarella. Season with cracked black pepper. Repeat the layers of Sugo, eggplant and cheeses until all the ingredients have been used.

Sprinkle the top with the breadcrumbs and bake for 20–25 minutes until golden brown and the cheeses have melted. Rest for about 15 minutes before serving.

* See Basics.

DEEP-FRIED CAULIFLOWER FLORETS

Cavolfiore fritti

Preparation time 5 minutes
Cooking time 25 minutes
Serves 4

1 medium-sized piece of cauliflower
6 eggs
salt and pepper to taste
200g (7 oz) flour
200ml (7 fl oz) olive oil

Wash the cauliflower and cut into florets.

Bring a medium-sized saucepan of water to the boil, add the cauliflower and cook for about 10 minutes. Drain and wipe dry with a clean tea towel (dish towel).

Whisk the eggs in a small bowl and season to taste. Place the flour in a separate small bowl. Dip the cauliflower into the flour and then the eggs.

Heat the oil in a frying pan over high heat and cook the cauliflower until golden brown. Drain on a paper towel and then serve hot.

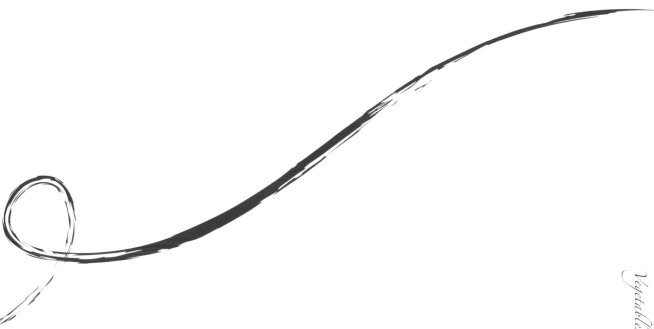

SALADS

Insalate

*M*eat dishes and summer lunches were always accompanied by one of Mum's insalate. There were hot salads and cold depending on the season, and the majority were green and "vegetabley" and were usually made with whatever we had growing in the backyard at the time.

The Sicilian salads were some of her best: sliced oranges with onions, salted sardines and old bread, the hot salad of potatoes, boiled eggs, rocket and pepper or her family-only recipe of shredded boiled pigs head with iceberg lettuce dressed only with lemon pepper and olive oil.

In good harvest months, there was a constant exchange of produce between our family and our uncles' and aunties' own gardens, so we were never short of variety. This generosity and love of fresh produce inspired us many years later when we opened the doors to Bertoni. We always have several fresh salads on the menu, and the number increases significantly over the summer months when people want more light and healthy lunch or dinner options.

RADICCHIO AND ROCKET SALAD
Insalata di radicchio e rugola

Preparation time 5 minutes
Serves 6

1 head radicchio (Italian chicory), leaves
   separated and finely shredded
2 large handfuls of wild baby rocket
4 tablespoons Olio Verde*
2 tablespoons Balsamic Vinegar del Modena*
large pinch of good-quality sea salt flakes
freshly cracked black pepper
plenty of freshly shaved parmesan cheese

Wash the radicchio and rocket and dry well.

   Combine the leaves in a large salad bowl. Add oil, vinegar, salt and pepper and toss to combine. Top with thinly shaved parmesan cheese and serve.

* See Basics.

CAPRESE SALAD

Insalata caprese

Preparation time 10 minutes
Serves 4

4 vine-ripened tomatoes, at room temperature
200g (7 oz) buffalo mozzarella cheese*
large pinch of good quality sea salt flakes
freshly cracked black pepper
6 tablespoons Olio Verde*
½ bunch baby basil leaves, whole
crusty bread, to serve

Slice the tomatoes ½ cm (¼ in) thick and arrange them in a circular pattern around a shallow serving platter. Tear the mozzarella (as you would a mandarin) and place on top of tomatoes. Season with sea salt flakes and freshly cracked black pepper. Drizzle with oil and garnish with basil leaves.

Allow to rest for 5 minutes before serving, as this allows the salt and oil to draw out the juices of the tomatoes.

Serve as a side dish with plenty of crusty bread to mop up all the delicious flavours.

* Buffalo mozzarella is available from good delicatessens.
** See Basics.

Salads

142

“My wonderful family brought me Bertoni's sage and pumpkin ravioli in hospital after the birth of my son. After four days of hospital food, I was craving some simple, delicious pasta; the ravioli hit the spot! The Bertoni's boys also shouted me a flat white with "Congratulations and Welcome, Baby Guiseppe (Joseph)" written on the side. Guiseppe has been Joseph's nickname ever since.”

Nicola

SPICY COUSCOUS AND ROAST VEGETABLE SALAD
Insalata di couscous e verdure al forno

Preparation time 20 minutes
Cooking time 20 minutes
Serves 6

1 packet couscous
2 tablespoons Moroccan spice*
1 tablespoon ground cumin
2 carrots, cut into batons
2 Spanish onions, cut into wedges
salt and pepper to taste
3 tablespoons vegetable oil
¼ bunch flat-leaf parsley, leaves picked

100g (3½ oz) rocket leaves
300g marinated roasted capsicums (bell
　peppers), thinly sliced
150g (5 oz) artichoke hearts, cut into quarters
125ml (½ cup, 4 fl oz) base dressing (see
　page 188)

Preheat the oven to 180°C (350°F, Gas Mark 4).

Combine the couscous, Moroccan spice and cumin in a large bowl and season to taste. Stir in enough boiling water to cover the couscous, cover with plastic wrap and leave to soak for 15 minutes or until the couscous has doubled in size. Run a fork through the couscous to loosen the ingredients, and set aside.

Place the carrots and onions on a flat baking tray, season to taste and drizzle with the vegetable oil. Roast in the oven until al dente, then set aside to cool.

To assemble the salad, add all the remaining ingredients to the couscous and mix through the dressing. Transfer to a shallow platter and serve.

* Moroccan spice is available from delicatessens and selected grocers.

BARLEY SALAD

Insalata di orzo

Pearl barley works well with this recipe as it soaks up the flavours of the other ingredients and the dressing. Pearl barley is relatively easy to cook so just follow the instructions on the packet.

Preparation time 15 minutes
Cooking time 15 minutes
Serves 6

2 zucchini (courgettes), cut into chunks
500g cherry tomatoes (about 2 small punnets)
3 tablespoons vegetable oil
salt and pepper to taste
1 cup barley, cooked according to packet
   instructions
¼ bunch mint, leaves picked
¼ bunch flat-leaf parsley, leaves picked

2 shallots or spring onions (scallions), thinly
   sliced
125g marinated eggplant (aubergine) strips,
   drained
125ml (½ cup, 4 fl oz) lemon dressing (see
   page 188)

Preheat the oven to 180°C (350°F, Gas Mark 4).

Combine zucchini, cherry tomatoes and oil in a bowl and season to taste. Transfer to a flat baking tray and roast in the oven until the zucchini are al dente and the tomato skins have split. Remove from oven and set aside to cool.

To assemble the salad, add all the remaining ingredients to the zucchini mix and toss the dressing through. Transfer to a shallow platter and serve.

CHICKEN AND PESTO PASTA SALAD

Insalata pasta-pollo

Basil oil is olive oil infused with fresh basil, which gives a subtle fresh flavour to a dish. You can buy basil oil at most gourmet food stores and selected grocers. Otherwise, you can make your own by placing 1½ cups fresh basil leaves, ¾ cup olive oil and ½ clove garlic in a food processor and pulsing until the basil is finely chopped.

Preparation time 15 minutes
Cooking time 15 minutes
Serves 4 as a meal or 6 as a side dish

300g (10 oz) chicken breast
salt and pepper to taste
2 tablespoons olive oil
500g (1 lb) pappardelle pasta
40ml (2 tablespoons, 1³/₅ fl oz) basil oil
50g (1¾ oz) wild rocket
200g (7 oz) semi-dried tomatoes

200g (7 oz) marinated artichoke hearts,
  drained and quartered
100g (3½ oz) pine nuts, toasted
80g (¾ cup, 2½ fl oz) pesto (see page 187)
salt and cracked black pepper to taste

Preheat the oven to 180°C (350°F, Gas Mark 4).

Season the chicken and then heat the olive oil in a frying pan, and sear both sides over high heat to seal. Transfer to a baking tray and cook in the oven for about 10 minutes. Cover loosely with foil and set aside to rest.

Cook the pappardelle according to the packet instructions. Drain, transfer to a large bowl and stir the basil oil through.

Slice the chicken and add it to the bowl with the pasta and the remaining ingredients, and season to taste with salt and cracked black pepper. Stir well to combine.

Note. This dish can be eaten warm or cold.

RISONI SALAD

Insalata alla Natale e Nicola

This dish is one that we make fresh in the shop every day. It came about when we were looking at alternative salad options. Natalie was a regular Bertoni customer and chef, and she came in to help us out when Claudio was on leave. Her husband Nick invented this recipe and, after some Bertoni fine-tuning, it has now become one of our most popular salads.

Preparation time 15 minutes
Cooking time 8 minutes
Serves 6

250g (8 oz) risoni pasta
10ml (2 teaspoons) lemon oil*
30ml ($^1/_8$ cup, 1 fl oz) lemon juice
3 teaspoons fresh marjoram, finely chopped
2 teaspoons Dijon mustard
½ teaspoon grated lemon zest
50ml ($^1/_5$ cup, 1 ¾ fl oz) olive oil
150g (5 oz) goat's cheese

2 shallots or green onions (scallions), thinly sliced
150g (5 oz) green Sicilian olives
salt and pepper to taste
60g (¼ cup, 2 oz) baby rocket leaves
125g cherry tomatoes, halved (approximately half a small punnet)

Cook the pasta according to the packet instructions. Drain and rinse under cold water until the pasta is cool. Transfer to large bowl and dress with lemon oil.

To make the vinaigrette, combine the lemon juice, 2 teaspoons of marjoram, the mustard and lemon zest in a small bowl and whisk. Add the olive oil and whisk until combined. Reserve 2 tablespoons of the vinaigrette. Add the remaining vinaigrette, cheese, green onions and olives to the risoni and toss to coat. Season to taste, cover and set aside to stand for 1–2 hours to allow the flavours to develop.

Note. At this point you can cover and refrigerate the salad for up to 24 hours. Once you continue to the next stage of the recipe, serve the salad immediately.

Add the reserved vinaigrette and the baby rocket leaves to the tomatoes, toss to combine and season to taste. Add the tomatoes to the risoni and toss to combine. Sprinkle the top with the remaining marjoram and serve.

* Lemon oil is available from gourmet food stores and selected grocers.

SWEETS AND COFFEE

Dolci e caffè

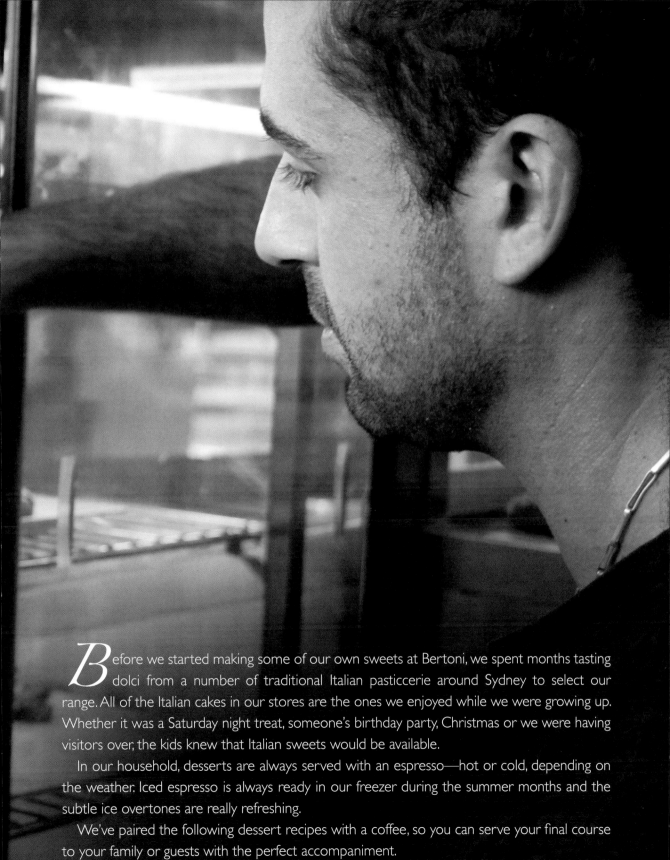

*B*efore we started making some of our own sweets at Bertoni, we spent months tasting dolci from a number of traditional Italian pasticcerie around Sydney to select our range. All of the Italian cakes in our stores are the ones we enjoyed while we were growing up. Whether it was a Saturday night treat, someone's birthday party, Christmas or we were having visitors over, the kids knew that Italian sweets would be available.

In our household, desserts are always served with an espresso—hot or cold, depending on the weather. Iced espresso is always ready in our freezer during the summer months and the subtle ice overtones are really refreshing.

We've paired the following dessert recipes with a coffee, so you can serve your final course to your family or guests with the perfect accompaniment.

Mamma's vanilla slices
Vaniglia fette alla Maria

Mum's been making this simple dessert for years, and she often brings a platter of slices into the store on weekends to give to our regular customers.

Preparation time 15 minutes plus cooling
Cooking time 15 minutes
Serves 6

2 sheets frozen puff pastry, thawed
400ml (13 fl oz) cream (single cream, half and half)
100g (3½ oz) vanilla instant pudding powder
icing sugar

Preheat oven to 180°C (350°F, Gas Mark 4).

Line 2 large baking trays (baking sheet, cookie sheet) with baking paper (baking parchment). Place a sheet of puff pastry on each baking tray and cover with another piece of baking paper. \Top with another baking tray to weigh it down and blind-bake until it is golden brown (approximately 15 minutes). Remove from the oven and set aside to cool at room temperature.

Whip the cream and pudding powder until the mixture thickens and soft peaks form. Place one cooked puff pastry sheet onto a tray. Spread the entire cream mixture evenly on the sheet. Top with other puff pastry sheet and slice into portions. Cover and refrigerate for 2 hours to overnight.

Dust with icing sugar and serve.

Pair with a cappuccino—espresso and 'stretched' milk (the technique used to froth the milk), topped with chocolate cocoa powder.

CLASSIC ITALIAN DESSERT

Tiramisu

This recipe can be made a day ahead but always tastes better when made on the day. Refrigerate after assembling. Remove from fridge at least 10 minutes before serving.

Preparation time 10 minutes
Serves 4

150ml (½ cup, 5 fl oz) cream (single cream, half and half)

3 tablespoons icing sugar (confectioners' sugar)

zest of 1 orange

250g (8 oz) mascarpone

250ml (1 cup, 8 fl oz) espresso coffee, cooled

2 tablespoons caster sugar (fine-grade granulated sugar)

8 savoiardi biscuits (ladyfingers)

150g (5 oz) dark chocolate, grated

Whip the cream, icing sugar and zest until soft peaks form. Fold in the mascarpone.

Put the coffee and the caster sugar into a shallow bowl and stir to combine. Dip the biscuits into the coffee mixture, coat both sides and remove quickly.

Cover the base of your serving dish (you can do individual serves or one larger size of an approximately 25 cm rectangle dish) with one layer of the biscuits. Follow with a layer of the cream mixture and a small amount of grated chocolate. Repeat these three layers until all ingredients have been used, topping with a layer of grated chocolate.

Pair with a macchiato—macchiato literally means 'stained or marked' so this coffee is an espresso topped with a stain of hot milk. Bertoni's version contains a little more milk.

MAMMA'S ALMOND BISCUITS
Amaretti di Mamma

Preparation time 10 minutes
Cooking time 6 minutes
Makes about 48 biscuits

500g (1 lb) caster sugar (fine-grade granulated
  sugar)
500g (1 lb) almond meal
20g (1 tablespoon, ½ oz) vanilla sugar
1 teaspoon vanilla extract
dash of almond essence (about ¼ teaspoon)
4 egg whites
100g (3½ oz) icing sugar (confectioners' sugar)
  plus extra for dusting

Preheat the oven to 160°C (325°F, Gas Mark 3).

Line a large baking tray (baking sheet or cookie sheet) with baking paper (baking parchment) and set aside.

In a large bowl, and using your hands, mix together the caster sugar, almond meal and vanilla sugar. Add the vanilla extract and almond essence. Add the egg whites gradually, making sure the mixture is not too wet. The mixture should come off your fingers clean and not sticky.

Sprinkle a generous amount of icing sugar on a clean work surface. Then, working with small portions of the mixture at a time, roll into a thin sausage shape, and place on the icing sugar. Thoroughly coat the sausage in the icing sugar and then cut the sausage into 2 cm (1¾ in) long pieces.

Stand the individual pieces upright, and gently press down and shape. Place onto the lined baking tray at least 2.5 cm (1 in) apart and bake for approximately 4–6 minutes. Biscuits are cooked when they just begin to crack.

Pair with an espresso—a traditional Italian shot of espresso coffee.

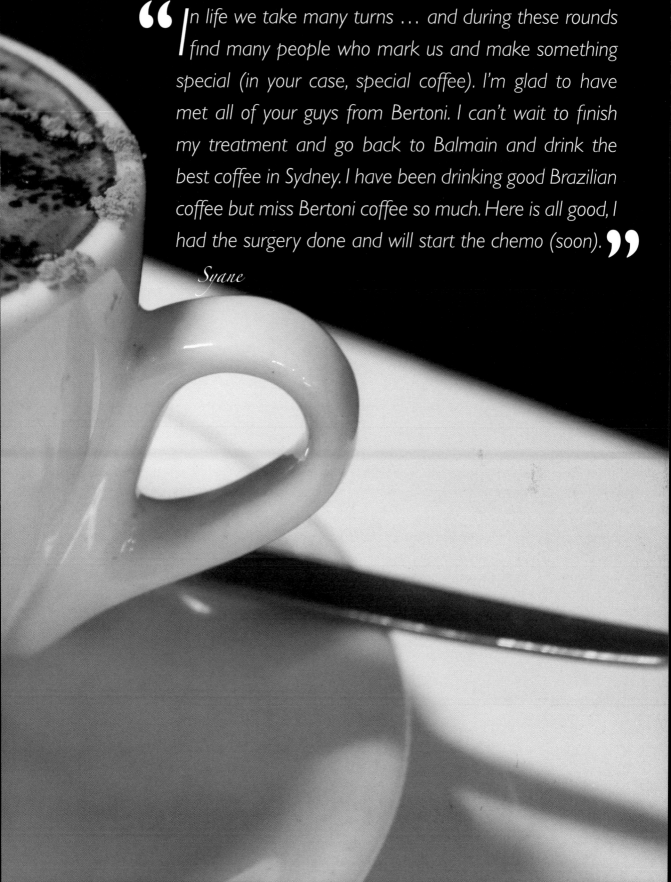

> "In life we take many turns … and during these rounds find many people who mark us and make something special (in your case, special coffee). I'm glad to have met all of your guys from Bertoni. I can't wait to finish my treatment and go back to Balmain and drink the best coffee in Sydney. I have been drinking good Brazilian coffee but miss Bertoni coffee so much. Here is all good, I had the surgery done and will start the chemo (soon)."
>
> *Syane*

CHOCOLATE BALLS

Palline di cioccolato

You can make these chocolate balls well ahead of time as they will last for more than a month in an airtight container in the refrigerator.

Preparation time 5 minutes plus refrigeration time
Cooking time 30 minutes
Makes about 50 balls

350g (12 oz) dark cooking chocolate
250g (8 oz) unsalted butter
250g (8 oz) icing sugar (confectioners' sugar)
2 egg yolks
110g (3½ oz) crushed almonds
125g (4 oz) roasted hazelnuts
chocolate sprinkles, to coat

Fill a medium-sized saucepan about 4 cm (1½ in) deep with cold water and bring to boil over medium heat. Reduce the heat to low and maintain a simmer. Place a heatproof bowl on top of the saucepan of simmering water.

Break up the chocolate and cut the butter into pieces, reserving 50g (1¾ oz) of the butter for later. Place both in the heatproof bowl, and stir continuously until they are melted and combined. When the ingredients have melted, remove from heat and set aside to cool. Add the icing sugar to the chocolate and combine. Then add the egg yolks and the crushed almonds, and mix well to combine. Place the bowl of chocolate mix in the freezer for about 20 minutes, stirring every 5 minutes, until the chocolate is firm but not frozen. Remove the mix from the freezer.

Spoon a small amount of the mixture into the palm of your hand and place 1 hazelnut in the centre of the mixture and shape into walnut-sized balls. Coat each ball in the chocolate sprinkles and place on a baking tray (baking sheet or cookie sheet) lined with baking paper (baking parchment).

Refrigerate for about 20–30 minutes before serving.

Pair with a mocha—espresso, chocolate syrup and stretched milk.

BERTONI'S FAVOURITE ITALIAN DOUGHNUTS
Ciambella alla sulfaro

We've been serving ciambella alla Nutella at Bertoni from the day we opened and they have become a signature sweet in our stores. These Italian-style doughnuts are best served either fresh or toasted crisp with a layer of Nutella through the centre. Often imitated but never duplicated, this ciambella recipe is from Pasticceria Sulfaro, the Haberfield institution of dolci, who kindly offered to share it with us.

Preparation time: 30 minutes plus resting time
Cooking time: 15 minutes
Makes approximately 17 ciambelle

1kg (2 lb) baker's flour, plus extra for dusting*
75g (2½ oz) yeast (fresh or dry)
10g (2 teaspoons, $^1/_3$ oz) salt
100g (3½ oz) margarine or unsalted butter
100g (3½ oz) caster sugar (fine grade
   granulated sugar) plus extra for coating
1–2 teaspoons vanilla extract
vegetable oil for deep frying
17 tablespoons Nutella

Combine the flour, yeast, salt, margarine, sugar and vanilla extract in a large bowl and mix to combine. Work the dough using your fingers until it becomes crumbly. Carefully and slowly add 550ml (19 fl oz) water, a little at a time, and knead the dough, tearing it apart and pushing it back together, until it is soft and moist. This kneading can take about 15–30 minutes (Iternatively you can prepare this recipe in an electric mixer).

Roll the dough into a ball and place it in a bowl that is big enough to allow the dough to rise. Cover the bowl first with a clean tea towel (dish towel) and then with a heavy towel (ensuring no air can get through) and set aside to rest for 15–20 minutes until it has slightly increased in size. As a guide, when you touch the dough before resting, it should feel stiff. When you touch the dough after resting, it should feel soft, and then it is ready to use.

Using a rolling pin, roll out the dough to about 1 cm (½ in) thick. Using two doughnut cutters, cut out each doughnut. Use a large cutter (around 6 cm, or 2¼–2½ in, in diameter) to cut the doughnut and a small one to cut out the doughnut hole.

Place each doughnut piece on a floured tray. Cover again with a clean tea towel (dish towel) and then a heavier towel (ensuring no air can get through) and leave to rest for 45 minutes to 1 hour, until the doughnuts have at least doubled in size. Your doughnuts are now ready to cook.

Note. If you wish, you can use the leftover dough from the doughnut holes by re-kneading and rolling the dough into a ball and repeating the process as above.

Fill a deep fryer with the oil and preheat to 180°C (350°F, Gas Mark 4).

Drop in the doughnuts 1–2 at a time, ensuring they do not touch each other, and fry for about 2–3 minutes until golden brown. Drain on paper towel and then coat in the extra caster sugar.

Tip: To ensure your doughnuts are light and fluffy, don't overknead or overflour your dough.
Tip: You can change the flavours of the ciambelle by replacing the vanilla extract with lemon, orange, almond extract or any other flavouring you wish.

Ciambella alla Bertoni

To make our variation of these doughnuts, slice each doughnut in half, add a good spread of Nutella straight from the jar, and put the two halves back together. To make the doughnut crispy, place between the sheets of baking paper (baking parchment) and toast in a sandwich press.

* Baker's flour is best used for breadmaking and has a higher gluten and protein content than plain flour. It's available from most gourmet food stores and selected grocers but you can substitute plain flour (all-purpose flour).

Pair with a Bertoni latte—double ristretto with about 2 inches of hot milk.

"What I love about Bertoni's is millions of things. One of the things I love is their amazing hospitality. My first year of school was the first year Bertoni opened … Always after a school day … we'll stop by and I'd grab a limonata from the fridge and Mum would get her coffee and says it's the best cup of coffee in the world. I'll give Antonio and Alberto a big high-five … Another thing I love is their exquisite Italian cuisine … probably half our fridge is chock full of Bertoni's amazing food."

Mitchell, aged 10

LEMON GRANITA

Granita di limone

Best made a day ahead.
Preparation time 5 minutes plus freezing time
Cooking time 5 minutes
Serves 6

130g (4½ oz) sugar
200ml (7 fl oz) freshly squeezed lemon juice

Heat 450ml (16 fl oz) water in a medium saucepan over medium–low heat without allowing it to boil. Add sugar and stir until dissolved. Remove from the heat and set aside to cool.

Add the lemon juice through a sieve and stir to combine.

Pour the mixture into a large freezer-proof tub and place it, uncovered, in the freezer. Remove the mixture from the freezer every 10 minutes and stir, repeating until the mixture begins to ice over. When the mixture begins to ice, stir it one last time, cover the tub with a lid and return it to the freezer for at least 3 hours before serving.

Serve a few tablespoons in a martini glasses before dessert or between courses to cleanse the palate. You could also top each glass with a teaspoon of chilled prosecco for a subtle and refreshing flavour.

Pair with 'the bomba'—Bertoni's version of the corretto, espresso with a shot of Dad's homemade brandy. Substitute with any good brandy or zambucca.

"Standing in the queue to buy coffee one day, I couldn't help but overhear the woman in front of me proceeding to tell Anthony about her dream the previous night—that she was lying on a table, head tilted back, with Anthony above her pouring coffee directly into her open mouth. Whoa! I suppose that has always been the charm of Bertoni for me—for a few minutes of your day, you can imagine you are somewhere else. Definitely in gorgeous Italy, in a busy local café, where the boys behind the counter flirt with you, have a joke with the blokes and give the kids a high-five. Helping the family is a friendly and likeable team and on Saturdays beautiful Nonna spreads her warmth and good cheer to all the customers handing out complimentary biscuits, and keeping her boys in check in case they get too cheeky. The food of course also feeds the soul—comforting and sustaining and at the same time, indulgent. In short, it is a warm, vibrant and inviting place to be."

Nadia

"We make it any way you like to drink it..."

Signature Bertoni Latte

OUR COFFEE
Il nostro caffè

We had our first cup of coffee before we were five years old, and we have been drinking it ever since. Mum used the traditional caffettiera to make espresso, and she delivered it to our bedside every morning before we even thought about breakfast. A latte macchiato was always served before bed (hot milk with a small amount of espresso, replaced with cold milk in the summer), which we would dip our savoiardi biscotti or Scotch Fingers into. After this we went straight to bed. We never had trouble sleeping, and still don't.

When we decided to open Bertoni, we spent more than six months working on the coffee until we were satisfied that we had achieved the same Italian flavour that you would get at any local café in Rome or Naples (or any other major Italian city).

We source our beans directly from the growers all over the world. We don't stick to one country, as harvests vary from season to season, so we buy from wherever the best beans are each time.

When the beans arrive in Australia, they're aged for a short time and roasted locally, artisan-style, in small batches by Gavin, who is our master roaster. The roasting process is long enough to maximise the concentrated flavour and aroma, but not so long that the caffeine is lost.

We serve only one blend of coffee at Bertoni, and it's a blend that we're proud of producing. It's mostly arabica beans mixed with the delicate robusta, and the flavour is full-bodied. Our decaf blend is made using the Swiss water process, so no chemicals are used to remove the caffeine.

Our baristas are trained by us personally to make sure that everyone makes coffee the same way. Our beans are freshly ground and our shots are made in double baskets so you get maximum coffee flavour per shot. The coffee machine is set to control the exact speed of the water passing through the 'group' (the machine's handle and coffee).

And our coffee philosophy is simple—we make it any way you like to drink it. We don't believe someone should pay more because they have an allergy to cow's milk and have to drink soy instead, or if you prefer your coffee extra strong, or even if you want a decaf.

Like the Italians, a good coffee is now part of Australian culture. Whether it's to kick-start your day, a midday pick-me-up or enjoyed with dessert at the end of a great meal, Australians have embraced the Italian coffee culture.

SAUCES AND DRESSINGS

Salse e condimenti

*M*ost typical Italian dressings are made with extra virgin olive oil, but Mum always preferred the light fruity flavour of olive oil or the subtlety of vegetable oil. Olive oil was as common as pasta back in Italy so, unlike the extra virgin variety, it was relatively cheap to buy. But in Sydney in 1956, it was hard to find. Mum used to buy it from a chemist in Newtown as this was the only place that she knew who sold it.

In our household, olive oil was generally used in cooking and either olive or vegetable oil was used to dress salads. But as we got older, our palates discovered the more delicate flavour of extra virgin olive oil and would often add it directly to a bowl of soup or pasta or dip some fresh ciabatta into it.

But oil discussions at our dinner table were never about the science that it is today. We never compared viscosity, acidity or fruit-to-skin ratios—it is, and has always been, just about taste and flavour.

BERTONI'S SECRET AÏOLI RECIPE

Aïoli alla Bertoni

We use our aïoli in salads and in our chicken schnitzel paninis as it adds a nice creamy texture with some subtle garlic mustard overtones. The trick to making a great aïoli is to mix vigorously the whole time and add the oil very slowly. This aïoli will keep in the refrigerator for at least a week if sealed in an airtight container.

Preparation time 10 minutes
Makes approximately 300ml (1¼ cups, 10 fl oz)

2 egg yolks
1 teaspoon Dijon mustard
¼ bulb garlic, roasted
2 tablespoons white wine vinegar
salt and white pepper to taste
250ml (1 cup, 8 fl oz) vegetable oil

In a food processor, process egg yolks, mustard, garlic and white wine vinegar, and seasoning to taste until well combined. While the processor motor is running, slowly pour in the vegetable oil until well combined. The aïoli should be a very thick consistency, like a mayonnaise. Once the right thickness has been achieved, add 1 tablespoon cold water to stabilise the aïoli. Transfer the aïoli to a clean jar, glass bowl or plastic container and seal with a lid or plastic wrap and refrigerate until required.

Tip. Never make aïoli with extra virgin olive oil as the flavour is too strong and will affect the creaminess.

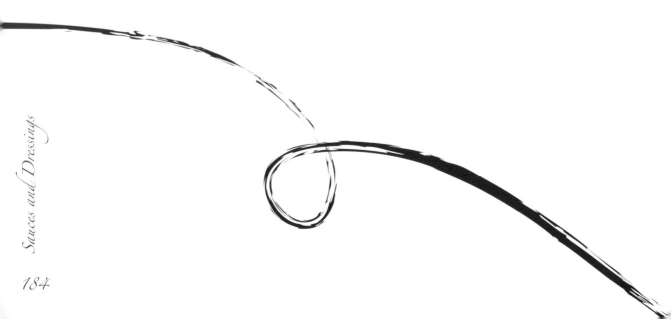

Bertoni's Secret Aïoli (page 184)
(Aïoli alla Bertoni)

BERTONI'S SECRET PESTO

Pesto di basilico

This pesto will keep in the refrigerator for at least a week if sealed in an airtight container.

Preparation time 15 minutes
Makes approximately 200ml

2 garlic cloves
50g (1 ¾ oz) pine nuts, lightly toasted
80g (7 tablespoons, 3 oz) basil leaves
4 tablespoons grated parmesan cheese
150ml (³/₅ cup, 5 fl oz) extra virgin olive oil plus
   extra for storing
1 teaspoon white wine vinegar

Put the garlic, pine nuts, basil and parmesan in a large mortar and pestle or a food processor and mix to make a paste. Add the oil in a slow and steady stream until combined. Stir in the vinegar. Transfer to a clean jar, glass bowl or plastic container and top with a layer of oil. Seal with a lid or plastic wrap and refrigerate until required.

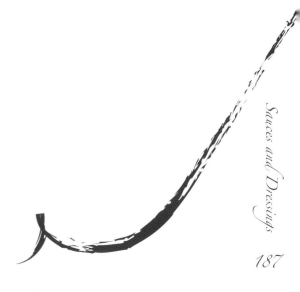

Sauces and Dressings

SALAD DRESSINGS

Condimenti

These four dressings are prepared in the same way, with all the ingredients simply whisked together. The base dressing can be used alone or you can add one of the other flavours below. Transfer the dressing to a clean jar, glass bowl or plastic container and seal with a lid or plastic wrap and refrigerate until required. All dressings will keep in the refrigerator for at least 1 week if sealed in an airtight container.

Preparation time 5 minutes
Each makes approximately 400ml (1¾ cups, 14 fl oz)

OLIO E ACETO (BASE DRESSING)
180ml (¾ cup, 6 fl oz) vegetable oil
180ml (¾ cup, 6 fl oz) white wine vinegar
1 tablespoon Dijon mustard
salt and ground white pepper to taste

MIELE DI STEPA (HONEY MUSTARD DRESSING)
180ml (¾ cup, 6 fl oz) vegetable oil
180ml (¾ cup, 6 fl oz) white wine vinegar
1 tablespoon Dijon mustard
1 tablespoon honey
salt and ground white pepper to taste

SEMI DI STEPA (SEEDED MUSTARD DRESSING)
180ml (¾ cup, 6 fl oz) vegetable oil
180ml (¾ cup, 6 fl oz) white wine vinegar
1 tablespoon good quality seeded mustard
salt and ground white pepper to taste

LIMONE E OLIO (LEMON DRESSING)
180ml (¾ cup, 6 fl oz) vegetable oil
180ml (¾ cup, 6 fl oz) lemon juice
1 tablespoon Dijon mustard
salt and ground white pepper to taste

"Each year during tomato season, our parents spend weeks making enough Sugo to last the rest of the year."

BASICS
Alimentari

These are basic pantry staples that are common in Italian cooking. We sell our own versions of these at Bertoni, but you can use any good-quality substitutes in our recipes.

Sugo del Giardino

This is a pasta sauce that has been in our family for generations. The base is simple but packed with flavour: you'll taste the sweetness of the tomatoes with every spoonful. Each year during tomato season, our parents spend weeks making enough Sugo to last the rest of the year. It takes them one full day to make just 50 jars. Not only do they supply our family with Sugo but they have been making Sugo for Bertoni since we opened.

Olio Verde

Olio Verde is made with Sicilian olives pressed green, which gives it a distinctive flavour unique in the olive family. Green olives are sweeter and fleshier than most varieties and produce a very high-quality oil. It contains delicate fruit, cut grass, black pepper and almond tones.

Balsamic Vinegar del Modena

Ours is a high-quality balsamic wine vinegar imported for Bertoni. It is concentrated from grapes cultivated in the Emilia Romagna region of Italy and aged in wooden casks for no less than two months.

Puttanesca sauce

Our puttanesca is a homemade, spicy sauce made with chilli, olives and other antipasto ingredients. It can be used as a base for pasta sauce or as a topping on some crusty Italian bread or crostini.

Dried pasta

Our dried pasta comes in two varieties—penne and fettuccine—and is restaurant quality made from durum wheat semolina. Using a good quality dried pasta makes a huge difference in the cooking process as the cheaper varieties can be sticky and more glutinous. The best way to cook pasta is al dente which means 'underdone'. It should be cooked so that it's firm but not raw.

You can buy all of our products in our cafés or order by email at contact@bertoni.com.au.

BERTONI
Casalinga

n. brothers Alberto (Bert) & Antonio (Toni);
Casalinga, adj. (home-made)

from Italy over 55 years ago, our parents
ught us that simplicity *(semplicita)* &
ess *(freschezza)* are key to great tasting
c Italian food. Over the years we shared
a feast *(festa)* with our family & friends
we want to share these flavours with y

er you're eating in *(per qui)*, taking it
portare via), standing up *(in piedi)*, o
the office *(a lavoro)*, our coffee, pani
i pasta & dolci will make you feel lik
our family *(famiglia)*.   *Buon Appet*

THE BERTONI STORY

La Storia di Bertoni

"When the final customer left and we closed the doors, we couldn't describe the high we felt."

OUR STORES
I Nostri Negozi

Bertoni Casalinga became the name of our store. It was our namesake—Bert and Tony—and Casalinga, or 'homemade', best described our offering of homemade Italian food.

After six months of renovations and getting council approvals, Bertoni Casalinga opened its doors on 31 July 2004. The piano accordionist played traditional tunes outside, an opera singer took stage on the communal table and silver and burgundy printed balloons covered the ceiling. The locals joined us in the hundreds to share in our opening celebrations and to taste some of our dishes and coffee.

At the end of the day, when the final customer left and we closed the doors, we couldn't describe the high we felt. We had been working sixteen to twenty hours every day in the lead-up to the opening, but for that moment, for that day-long party, it was all worth it. And then reality hit—we had to do this all again tomorrow, and the day after that, and the day after that … this was our new life. The thought was both exhausting and exhilarating at the same time, but we knew we were ready for the challenge.

Within the first year we attracted many visitors as well as the locals, many of whom, we discovered, travelled from the north side of Sydney. So when the old Dip Café became available on Vista Street in Mosman, we decided it was a good place for a second Bertoni store. We had enough family involved in the business to staff another store, and so on 5 August 2006 Bertoni Due opened its doors. Many regular Balmain customers came to join in the celebrations and the locals welcomed us to the community.

Our sister Luisa works at the Mosman store almost every day now, after giving up her role as a consultant accountant. Not many people know this, but Luisa is actually a silent partner in the Bertoni business. Which basically means that she 'donated' some money to her brothers for the start-up, we get our BAS prepared for free and she has a job for life.

The city store came next, which was again seeded by our customers, many of whom worked in the CBD during the week. We had already established a catering client base in the CBD too so it made sense to look for a place there. And so on 14 January 2008 another Bertoni was born. Meren, who had been working with us in Balmain, took over the reins in the city store and welcomed all the local white-collars in for their daily coffee and food.

While each of our stores is unique in its own way, we've tried to maintain some of the key Bertoni-isms such as the food, the blackboard menus, our family and the milk crates that are used for seats, which inadvertently have became synonymous with our name.

Bert and Tony

"To this day, before we go to work, we still say 'have fun today' to each other."

A sister's perspective ...

When Berto and Tony came to me and told me of their plans to open an Italian café, I thought they were insane. Sure, we all understood great Italian food, but they both had only corporate experience in other industries. I decided to invest in the business solely because I wanted to minimise their financial loss, because I feared they would lose everything. I offered them my services as an accountant for free (a decision I have come to regret every day of my life since!) and became a silent partner.

Bertoni Balmain opened on 31 July 2004 with the whole family in attendance. I remember blowing up balloons with my sisters-in-law, and the excitement that was building amongst us as we counted down to the official opening of the Bertoni doors. Mum and Dad had never stood prouder as they watched us. There was probably an even greater excitement for Mum as she had developed all the recipes and assisted in the cooking of all the foods on offer. She could not wait to see the expressions on everyone's faces as they savoured the dishes. There were queues all down Darling Street that day, as people patiently waited to taste the food that Mum was giving away. This tradition has continued to date—we encourage all of our customers to taste our food before they buy.

I remember just before we opened the doors Tony saying 'whatever happens today, let's just remember to have fun' and that we did. To this day, before we go to work, we still say 'have fun today' to each other. Not often do you have the opportunity to work in a business where every day is filled with interesting people who visit us and teach us about life. From day one, Bertoni was always an extension of our home, and our customers have become our extended family.

When the Mosman café opened in August 2006, I was concerned about how the locals would receive us, because we didn't really know the area. I quickly realised that people are the same wherever you go. They have the same concerns about life, love, family, health and the world. We learnt from our parents when we were very young that if you treat people with respect and welcome them wholeheartedly into your home they cannot help but respond positively. We hold this value dear to our hearts, and we have always applied this principle in all of our stores.

We were always close growing up, but we became extremely close as a family unit after the loss of my brother Angelo in 1978. Bertoni has given our family the excuse we all needed to ensure that we are a part of each other's lives every day. Rarely does a day pass that we do not communicate. For that I am truly grateful.

Luisa

"We've watched newborns grow into young children and teenagers graduate from school."

OUR CUSTOMERS
Il Nostri Cliente

From the beginning, the Balmain locals embraced our family affair. Most of our original regulars still visit us every single day and many have become friends of the famiglia.

Before we came to know everyone's name, we quickly learned their coffee and food habits. Like macchiato with just a measured amount of milk, who rides in on his motorbike first thing in the morning. We hear his bike coming so his coffee is ready to drink as soon as he walks through the door.

A somewhat impatient customer loiters at the front waiting for the doors to open so he can get his long black with four. He often returns during the day for another coffee or a bottle of Coke and we never charge him. Mick is one of the local homeless guys in Balmain.

Large flat white has hers with either honey or two sugars (depending on the batch of honey). Jacinta loves her Bertoni coffee so much, she dropped in to grab one on her way home 22 hours after giving birth to Freddy.

Large latte with two sugars, cold milk and chocolate on top comes in most days and she remembers everyone's birthday. Carly orders her coffee with a side of honesty, telling any one of us if we're getting too fat or looking tired.

Strong flat white enjoys her daily coffee with a side of a couple of bungers (cigarettes), but we won't tell her husband Greg. She comes in for breakfast with Greg some mornings too (minus the bungers). We've become friends with Kath and Greg now and look forward to our annual movie night at the open-air cinema.

And anyone who comes to Bertoni will often see the movie stars, rock legends and celebrated chefs who visit on a regular basis. They mix in seamlessly with the locals and love the fact that they can remain relatively anonymous when they come into the store. Master chef can marry the most unusual ingredients to make world-class dishes but he still likes to come to Bertoni for his toasted panino and short black. Well-known actor couple come in regularly for their lattes and osso bucco. International movie legends like their flat whites with skim, and Oscar-winning American actor has an Americana when he's in town, which we came to learn is a long black.

These are just a few of the customers and orders that we have come to know. We've met literally thousands of people who come for food and coffee and stay on to share their lives with us on a daily basis. We've seen singles find love, couples get married and sadly, even divorced. We've watched newborns grow into young children and teenagers graduate from school. We've been a part of the highs and lows of all our regular customers' lives.

On the flip side, they've also come to know us and have become a part of our daily lives. They live through Albert's morning sweats, Anthony's no-discount policy, Johnny's Aussie-fied 'seenyora' greetings, the boys' unsavoury Movember mos, our first favourite café award and Mum's weekly biscotti tasting.

And we wouldn't want it any other way. To all of our customers we say 'grazie mille'.

"We have found plenty of diamonds that have worked, and still work with us today."

OUR STAFF
Il Nostro Staff

OK, I'll say it. And I don't believe anyone who operates a business in hospitality will disagree: staff is the most challenging side of the business. Finding them, getting them to work when you need them and keeping them for longer than their university holiday is an ongoing cycle.

When we first opened Bertoni in Balmain, we had everyone in the family who was old enough to work on the roster. Which was great, because it meant that for the most part, we didn't have to worry about someone not showing up to work, leaving early or even paying them for that matter. Ah, you gotta love family.

But we did need to recruit some key people to help us get started. We found Claudio, who said he applied for the job because he loved the quote we had written at the end of the ad—'rompa palle non applicare' which essentially means 'ball-breakers need not apply'. Claudio hails from Sicily, not far from my father's village, and his speciality is making traditional Sicilian food with whatever ingredients you give him. Claudio worked with our Mum in the kitchen for almost three years, before moving on to chase his own dreams.

Then we found Kathy, who has been a barista with us from day one, and only departed recently to have her second child. Her husband, Nick, wants her to be a stay-at-home mum, but we're hoping to see her back as soon as baby number two can say 'Dad, milk'.

Charlie was a mate who came to help out one day and ended up staying with us for about nine months. We're not sure if we ever paid him for his efforts and we always wondered why it took him two hours to find the coffee cups in our storeroom. But he kept showing up so we kept giving him things to do. He moved on to a paying job, first as our coffee rep and then our dolci rep, before starting his own catering business.

Apart from a few other transients, that was the original Bertoni team.

Since then, and outside of the challenge of weeding through the rough, we have found plenty of diamonds that have worked, and still work with us today. They have become part of the Bertoni family and, honestly, we don't know what we'd do without them.

OUR THANKS
I Nostri Grazie

This book has been years in the mind and months in the making and there are a few key people we need to acknowledge and thank for their help in putting it together.

Thanks to Danny Russo, who is one of our closest and dearest friends. Thanks a lot mate for sharing some of your signature recipes in this book.

Thanks to Guiseppe from Pasticceria Sulfaro for sharing your family recipe of one of our most popular dolci—ciambella.

Thanks to Natalie for all your help testing the recipes and working with us during the book's production. We came to know you as a customer, but we're proud to have you as a friend.

Thanks to Mina, Tony's wife, for working on this book. This book was her idea, her project and, without her months of hard work and focus, it wouldn't have happened.

And of course to our Mamma Maria and Papa Alfonso who developed our palates and inspired all the flavours of Bertoni. Thanks for everything you do for us every day and for finally writing down some of your wonderful recipes. We love you so much and would not know what we would do without you both.

And to those who didn't contribute to the book but who contribute significantly in the day-to-day running of our business: Greg (or Craig as Mum likes to call him), our friendship started with that contra-deal of your fixing our sound system in return for a case of Mamma's sugo, and now you've become one of the family. We can't thank you enough for everything you do for us.

George, you may be a professional in commercial refrigeration and air conditioning, but somehow you became our general fix-it man too. Our food just wouldn't be cold without you, so thanks for everything.

John, we met you more than seven years ago when you came to our home to fix the plumbing and extract the earring that had been dropped down the sink. You're the most generous and honest plumber we've ever met. Thanks for always getting us out of trouble.

George, thanks for the souvlaki dinners and for always keeping our cars safely on the road. We really appreciate all you do for us and we value your friendship.

Thanks to Josh for looking after our stairs, driveway, shelving, signage and for always being willing to help with anything and everything we've needed. You're a good bloke.

Thanks to Albert's wife Maura who made it possible for Albert to show up for work.

Of course, we have to say a huge thank you to all of our loyal customers, staff, suppliers, family and friends for your ongoing and continued support and for sharing in the family that is Bertoni. There are too many of you to list here individually but we hope you know that we appreciate you and Bertoni wouldn't exist without you.

Thanks to Muriel from Blue-Eyed Dragon for introducing us to your friend Fiona. And last but not least thanks to Fiona from New Holland for making our book. I hope you're as proud of it as we are.

'*Simply the best café…*' Sydney Morning Herald Good Food Guide

'*authentic Italian-Australian exuberance and excellent coffee…*'
Simon Thomsen/Joanna Savill, Sydney Morning Herald Good Food Guide

'*An experience I will never forget…*' Sydney Coffee Guide

'*…Bertoni's family-run business again takes first prize for NSW…*' Delicious Magazine

'*…the atmosphere is canteen chic, warmed by the glow of la Mamma*'
Helen Greenwood, Sydney Morning Herald

'*…the best sugo in Australia*' Steve Jacobs, Channel 9 Today Show

'*…the coffee was simply spectacular*' Sydney Coffee Guide

'*…one of Sydney's best cafes*' Delicious Magazine

'*…a solid & generous menu that keeps everyone entertained…*'
Simon Thomsen/Joanna Savill, Sydney Morning Herald Good Food Guide

'*…the food is seriously good*' Sydney Eats

'*…a new favourite with locals*' Vogue Entertainment & Travel

BERTONI *Casa*

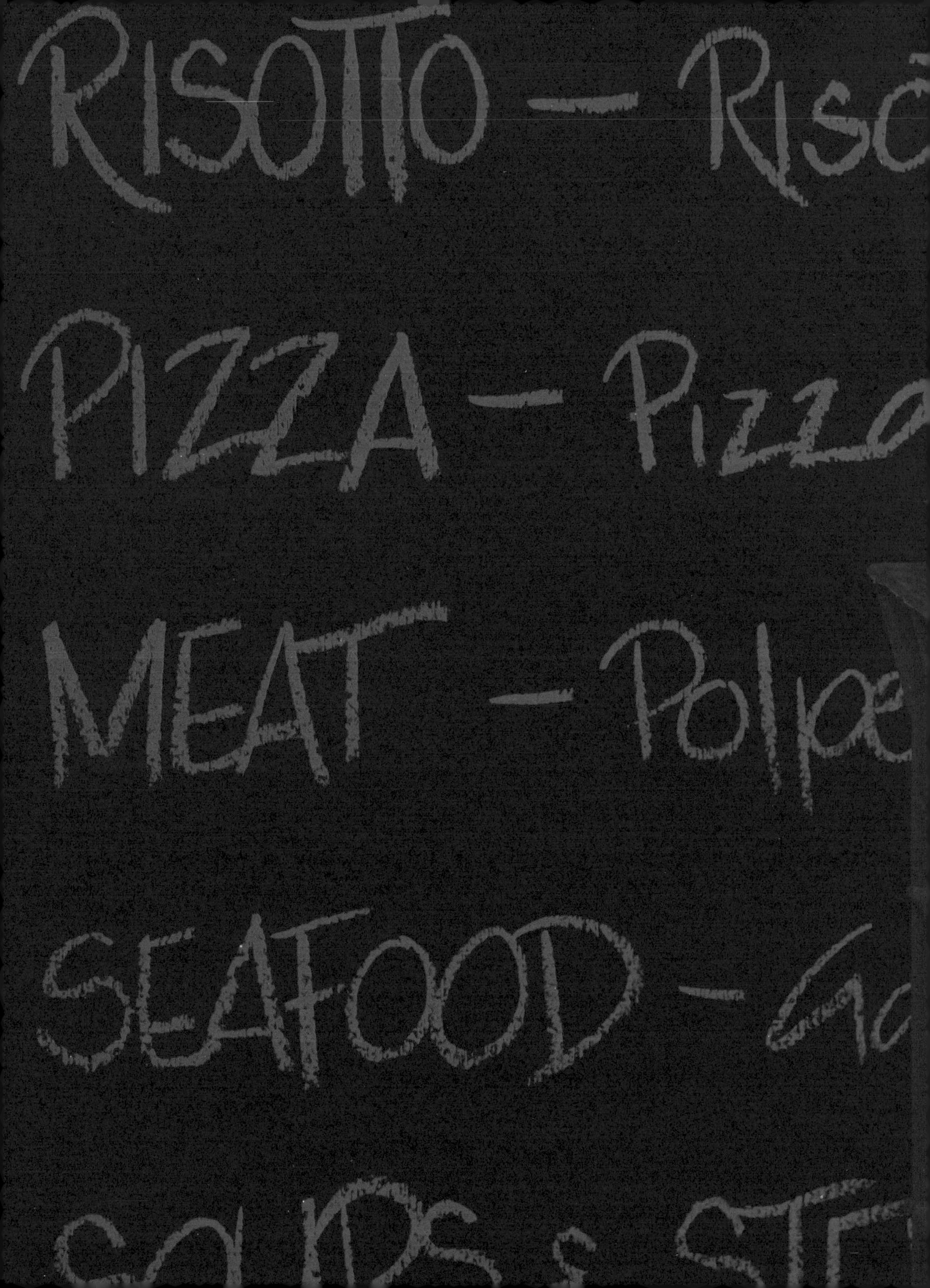

RISOTTO — RISO

PIZZA — Pizza

MEAT — Polpe

SEAFOOD — Go

SOUPS & STE